Always Now

Collected Poems
Volume Two

Always Now

Volume One (2003)
From Elsewhere
Winter Sun
The Dumbfounding
Translations

Volume Two (2004)
sunblue
No Time

Volume Three (for release in 2005)
Not Yet But Still
Concrete and Wild Carrot
Too Towards Tomorrow: New Poems

Margaret Avison
Always Now ⫷

The Collected Poems
Volume Two

The Porcupine's Quill

Library and Archives Canada Cataloguing in Publication Data

Avison, Margaret, 1918–
Always now : collected poems / Margaret Avison.

ISBN 0-88984-262-0 (V. 1) – ISBN 0-88984-255-8 (V. 2)

I. Title.

PS8501.V5A17 2003   C811'.54   C2003-902232-3
PR9199.3.A92A17 2003

Published by The Porcupine's Quill, 68 Main St, Erin, Ontario NOB 1TO.
http://www.sentex.net/~pql

Readied for the press by Stan Dragland and Joan Eichner.
Copy edited by Doris Cowan.

Represented in Canada by the Literary Press Group.
Trade orders are available from University of Toronto Press.

We acknowledge the support of the Ontario Arts Council and the Canada
Council for the Arts for our publishing program. The financial support of the
Government of Canada through the Book Publishing Industry Development
Program is also gratefully acknowledged. Thanks, also, to the Government
of Ontario through the Ontario Media Development Corporation's Ontario
Book Initiative.

Canada Council
for the Arts

Conseil des Arts
du Canada

Canadä

ONTARIO ARTS COUNCIL
CONSEIL DES ARTS DE L'ONTARIO

Volume Two

A Note on the Text

The three volumes of *Always Now* contain all of Margaret Avison's
published books of poetry. The author has removed a very few poems:
'Public Address' (from *Winter Sun*), 'The Two Selves' and 'In
Eporphyrial Harness' (from *The Dumbfounding*), 'Highway in April,'
'The Evader's Meditation,' and 'Until Christmas' (from *sunblue*), 'Living
the Shadow,' 'Insomnia' and 'Beginning Praise' (from *No Time*),
'Having Stopped Smoking' and 'Point of Entry' (from *Selected Poems*).
The opening section of volume one, 'From Elsewhere,' is arranged
according to date of publication, from 1932 to 1991, the date of *Selected
Poems*. 'From Elsewhere' includes the 'Uncollected' and 'New Poems' of
that book, except for the two noted above and 'The Butterfly,' which is
here in its original form. All of the poems in *Always Now* having been
considered and reconsidered, and small corrections having been made,
the book contains definitively all of the published poems up to 2002
that Margaret Avison wishes to preserve.

sunblue ⫷

Sketches

Thaws

The snowflow
nearly-April releases   melting bright.

Then a darkdown
           needles and shells the pools.

Swepth of suncoursing sky
steeps us in
         salmon-stream
             crop-green
                rhubarb-coloured shrub-tips:

everything waits for the
lilacs, heaped tumbling – and their warm
licorice perfume.

Weekend

On the hall-table a safetypin

under the

small brass fern pot with its

artificial fern.

No dust

but no smell of cooking;

the carpet's corner's curled.

Overcast Monday

In this earth-soakt air
we engage with
undeathful technicalities,
hurt that they click.

An oil of gladness, in
the seafloor Light
quickens, secretly.

A Work Gang on Sherbourne and Queen, Across from a Free Hostel for Men

The hostel's winter flies
where morning spills them out
fumble, undisturbed
by street or curb;

paralleled, walled off, by the force
of the through north-south route,
they never meet
the yellow-helmeted men across the street
whose tangling ways, among
dump trucks and crane scoops, put
down, solid and straight,
the new storm sewer conduit.

Both groups go zigzag, veer,
        stand, wait –

but not the same.

Sketches

18

Cement Worker on a Hot Day

I've passed this yellow hydrant
in sun and sleet, at dusk –
             just a knob
                shape.

Now, here, this afternoon
suddenly a man
stops work on the new curb in
the oils of sun,

                  and (why of course!)
                  wrenches the hydrant till
                  it yields a gush
                  for him to gulp and wash in.

Yes   yes   a hydrant
was always there but now
it's his,   and flows.

A Childhood Place

In the mattressed pasture the
sun's butterfat
     glistens on coarse grass.

    The grassblades scrape.

        Seashells of my scattered years
        whiten in the sun.

On the weathered door
wood-hairs leave shadow-lines on the
hot wood.

                              Sketches

CNR London to Toronto (i)

Grasses bronze and tassel-tawny
knock-kneed trees in little orchard
picnic table frozen in a
backyard tilt beside a thorny
brushheap somebody will burn
with orange flame and lilac smoke
against a cold blue-and-white sky
some day after the train has long
since fled with us
           and lost
these morning places.

CNR London to Toronto (ii)

In the Christmas tree and
icing sugar country
they listen under banks
badger foreheads sleek
the sun uncaring, frost
squeaky, bright with
berries: *invisibility*.

From a Train Window
(Leamington to Windsor) in March

Miles of beeswax mist,
    a far ravine with fishbone trees,
        one nearer, peacock's quill-fan with
        the violet batik faintly suggested
            by springtime leaflessness;
    rust-spotted   chipped-paint places,
        roadshoulder, gas-pumps,   and a
            flagless metal flagstick;
    somebody's bricks stashed under tarpaulins,
        a wooden bridge in a field and a black
        dog pottily floundering across it:

the pale wintergreen air has
straw stuck to it, and then again becomes
    dimmed in beeswax mist, a
    visual amplitude so still
        that you can hear the hidden culvert gurgle.

The Seven Birds (College Street at Bathurst)

Storm-heaped west, wash-soaked with
dayspill.   Light's combers
broken, suds-streaming
                    darkwards and stormwards:

          rough roofs
          two-story store flats
          false gables and futile
      T V aerials   high wire time and
             nobody home yet –
      the stormy sunlit evening children
          whirl with the grit
          and the candy-wrapper gusts
      right by the gridwork flow on rails and wheels, under
                                   the very shadow of
      heaven and the heavy
      trampling home-bent crowds,
          hoping for supper.

      Seven birds toss
      skyward and glide
      and ruffle down:

          birds on the T V wires
      eye-mirroring the light of the
          wild west.

The floods of blackness
swirl (bells and pomegranate pompoms) in.

End of a Day *or* I as a Blurry

I as a blurry groundhog bundling home
find autumn storeyed:

> underfoot is leafstain and gleam of wet;
> at the curb, crisp weed
> thistled and russeted;
> then there's the streetlight level;
> then window loftlights, yellower;
> above these, barely, tiers
> of gloaming branches,
> a sheet of paraffin-pale wind,
> then torn cloud-thatch and
> the disappearing clear.

Indoors promises
such creatureliness as disinhabits
a cold layered beauty
flowing out there.

Grass Roots

There is a grass-roots level:
small ears and weed-stems;
necklacing ant-feet; robins' toe-pronging and beak-thrust;
raindrops spotting in,   or
cratered, sluicing, and wrenching
grass flat, gouging
earth, to enrich.

Summer is so.

Winters, that level
is ore, deep under snow.

Stone's Secret

Otter-smooth boulder
lies under rolling
black river-water
stilled among frozen
hills and the still unbreathed
blizzards aloft;
silently, icily, is probed
stone's secret.

Out there – past trace
of eyes, past these
and those memorial skies
dotting back signals from
men's made mathematics (we
delineators of curves and time who are
                            subject to these) –
out there, inaccessible
to grammar's language the
stones curve vastnesses,
cold or candescent
in the perceived
processional of space.
                         The stones out there in the
                         violet-black are part of a
                         slow-motion fountain? or of a
                         fireworks pin-wheel?
                         i.e. breathed in and out
                         as in cosmic lungs? or
                         one-way as an eye looking?
What mathematicians must,
also the pert,
they will
as the dark river runs.

Word has arrived that
peace will brim up, will come
'like a river and the
glory … like a flowing stream.'
So.
Some of all people will
wondering wait
until this very stone
utters.

Hid Life

Red apples hang frozen
in a stick-dry, snow-dusty
network of branches,
against lamb's wool and pastelblue of sky,
a crooked woodenness, a wizening red.

Are these iron stems? or is
this tree in a lee out of the
clattering winds?

Heavily in my heart
the frost-bruised fruit, the sombre tree,
this unvisited room off winter's endless corridors
weigh down.

        But
even this fruit's flesh
will sodden down at last.

Botanist, does the seed
so long up held
still somehow inform
petal and apple-spring-perfume
for sure, from so far?

Is the weight only
a waiting?

Released Flow

In the sunward sugarbush
runnels shine and down-rush
through burning snow and thicket-slope.
The spiced air is ocean-deep.

Melting ridge and rivermouth
shape the waters in the earth
and the motions of the light
close the flow as watertight.

                  'In and out the windows'
                  squirrels flip and play
                  through sunsplash and high and low
                  in winter's gallery.

The extraordinary beyond the hill
breathes   and is   imperturbable.
Near the gashed bough the hornets fur
in paperpalace-keep and -choir.

Across snowmush and sunstriped maples
honeyed woodsmoke curls and scrolls.
Sunblue and bud and shoot wait to unlatch
all lookings-forth, at the implicit touch.

March Morning

The diamond-ice-air is ribbon-laced
with brightness.   Peaking wafering snowbanks are
sun-buttery, stroked by the
rosy fingertips of young
tree shadows
as if for music;
and all the eyes of God glow, listening.

My heart branches,
swells into bud and spray:
heart break.

The neighbour's kid
lets fall his mitts
shrugs jacket loose
and wondering   looks   breathing the
crocus-fresh   breadwarm
        Being –
easy as breathing.

March

A Caribbean airflow
shampoos the brook.
The deepsea deepwarm look of
sky wakes green below
amid the rinds of snow.

Though all seems melt and rush,
earth-loaf, sky-wine,
swept to bright new horizons
with hill-runnel, and gash,
all soaked in sunwash,

far north, the ice
unclenches, booms
the chunks and floes, and river brims
vanish under cold fleece:
the floods are loose!

Then sullen torn
old skies through tattery trees
clack, freezing
stiffens loam; the worn
earth's spillways then relearn
                    how soaring bliss
                    and sudden-rigoring frost
                    release
                    without all lost.

Let Be

Behind the rainmurk
is, I persuade myself,
a mountain shouldering
near enough   one might mark
– but for the rain – the treeline
from the implausible plateau of this
Parisgreen cow pasture
watered by a
meander (old river now a
ditch brimming over into
frog-marsh), this side of
the massive roots
of light,   of rain,   of
mountain-range.

Let there be
splashings, shouts,
dogs gnawing, oarlocks,
or people's random opinions
on a battery radio,
or the precise   other   inevitable
alternative – as will be plain –
to give ballast in daylight
to the unseen mountain's
no-sounding soundness.

Water and Worship: An Open-air Service
on the Gatineau River

On the pathway mica glints.
Sun from the ripple-faceted water
shines, angled, to grey cliffs and the blue sky:
    from up here the boat-braided river is
    wind-riffled, fishes' meadows.
                    But at
        eye level, on the dock, the water looks deep,
                cold, black, cedar-sharp.
        The water is self-gulping under
        clefts and pier posts.

We listen.
Your all-creating stillness, shining Lord,
trembles on our unknowing
          yearning
              yielding lives:
    currents within us course
    as from released snow, rock-
    sluiced, slow welling from
          unexpected hidden springs,
    waters still acid,
    metallic with old wrecks –
        but Love draws near,
        cut-glass glory, shattering everything
                  else in
        the one hope known:

        (how are You so
        at home with what we know?)

The waters lap.
Rocks contain and wait
in the strong sun.

       'Joyful, joyful, we adore Thee....'

Sounds Carry

Nimbus of summer
undefines place and
time imitates an immemorial dawn
                              – dogs at the white gates....
Breathing is palpable, and
breathes response to amplitude
and hidden tendril,
yearning for large and little;
and calm birds pick about their toes
or settle, riffling, down.

Misty summer
sidetracks years
to disused loading sheds sweet with the
sun on worn boards ... flies
and bird cheepings ...
a clarity beyond the mist
within the nimbus of this summer's now.

Thirst

In the steeped evening
deer stand, not yet
drinking
beyond the rim of here;

and crystal blur
clears to the jet
stream, pure, onflowing:
a not yet known –

beyond the grasses where the deer

stand, deep in evening
still.

'While as yet no leaves may fall'

(William Barnes)

I came on a spare corner in time,
an empty angle, in a broken light;
the sound of voices from committee-rooms
came distantly (like the irrelevant
clatter at noon in hospital hallways
to the patient immured in the last
lucid wash of light).   From somewhere near
pigeons were burbling, and motors sighed,
but only soughed the surface.

                 The back stairs
in old farmhouses create space like this.

In the wayside chapel a stiff bunch of
an old bouquet rustles to the wind.

The evening meadows wait   under the willow trees.

Morning Bus

A bird is flattened on the road's shoulder.
The feathers fibrillate
as the slowed bus sighs.

Through the bus's gills
the nearing lake air
breathes in. We breathe:

something is, nonetheless, foul –
fish in the stew of time
flaked, on green sand? the
bulky buildings sweating rancid stove oil?

The feathers flutter
on unflyable wings
wadded in morning-drying clay.

We breathe.
We jolt. This slump of letting be
refuses fusion; it is a
non-homogeneity that goes on.

For each, enough
is destination.

A Lament

A gizzard and some ruby inner parts
glisten here on the path where wind has parted
the fall field's silken ashblonde.

I fumble in our fault
('earth felt the wound,' said Milton).
Cobwebs of hair glued
to cheekbone, among
gnat eddies and silences,
I clamber on through papery leaves and slick
leathering leaves between
the stifling meadows.

Eyeblink past blue,   the far
suns herd their flocks.

Crumbling comes,
voracious, mild as loam –
but not restoring.   Death has us glassed in
for all the fine airflow and the
auburn and wickerwork beauty of this valley.

Somewhere a hawk swings, stronger,
or a weasel's eyes brighten.

The viscera still shine
with sun, by weed and silver riverflow.

On?

There is a direction? And it's
   on?
          Toughly and cheerily
          the pathfinders encourage
          at the last stepping-stone
                  ('There
                      we are!')

If it is on, then
   where we know, or
   where we're going to,
      is all one?

Yoo hoo.
Dark.   A whiplash branch – I'm holding it – are you
                            there?
   Whose
   breathing?
   (No one's?)
No no no. No
more, I don't like being left
      alone like this.

On is the planet's –
earth-rush, girth-swivel, candlepower to the nth –
   not mine. I
   lie brambled biting on a
          root.
   Wait!   Wait for whoever (me?)
     is out here in this
     thickety wild place!

O day breaking – away down engraved and embossed on the
        sheen of water:
                        On would've been O V E R I tell you. I
                        hung on to this wind-ragged tag of a
                        bush, not-going in time – it's the
                        sheer edge almost.   I hung
'On?'
        Yes.

A Work-Up

THE ANGEL OBSERVES

> lips, as if stone-carved,
> cold, the grit lying unfanned and
> sand-dry – an engine-hood of a
> cathedral, cabaret spotlights –
> moving to speak....

THE ANGEL ENTERS.

> (Mildly):
> > 'What *are* you about?
> > You're itting yourself.'

> (The wind suspires.)

> The astonied eyelids
> fail even to blink.

THE ANGEL BEGINS TO LEAVE:

> 'Wind and light want to be bare
> to your unringing ear,
> beloved. Oh, beware!'

Contemplatives *or* Internal Combustion

Around 4 a.m.
the hermits come
and gun a jalopy
apiece down the empty
unseen car-track

past the sealed air-controlled
night-hollowed office blocks
and jumbled dormitory blocks
with windows hoisted up
and blinds tap tapping.

Deadly down these
roofless tunnels the hermits
clatter and boom,
spanging bullets of sound
around and further away
and away.

By busying 6 a.m.
out along ditch canals
beyond the horsefarms and the mushroom sheds
under the chassis they sleep
or over the wheel
waiting out daylight-solitude,
getting set to rev up,
again.

Technology Is Spreading

Two men hatless plodding
behind, in the rain,
one to the other confiding,
set this strategem:
    'When using a
    computer it is always desirable
    to stick to one language.'

'These words,' said memory,
'have come unsung –
but note (in case of "always"
or too many a sticky tongue).'

And yet, one 'stuck' to
who could 'desire'?
Just today's luck to
so catch unfire.

Two men, one fair-haired
one nearly bald
passed unimpaired had
while the rain squalled.

Strong Yellow, for Reading Aloud

written for and read to English 389's
class when asked to comment on my
poem 'The Apex Animal', etc.

A painted horse,
a horse-sized clay horse, really,
like blue riverclay, painted,
with real mural eyes – or a
Clydesdale with his cuff-tufts
barbered – the mane
marcelled like a conch and cropped and plastered down like a
merry-go-round pony's
without the varnish –
all kinds confounding,
yet a powerful presence
on the rainy Sunday diningroom wall,
framed by a shallow niche ...

Q: 'Miss Avison could you
        relate that to the "head of a horse"?'

No. No. That one
was strong yellow – almost tangerine, with
white hairs, the eyes
whited too as if
pulled back by the hair
so the eyeballs would water with wind in them,
one you'd call Whitey, maybe,
though he was not, I say,
white ...

Q: 'Auburn?'

It was not a horse-shaped horse,
or sized. It loomed. Only the

narrow forehead part, the
eyes starting   loose and appled,
and shoulder-streaming part ...
Colour? a stain on the
soiled snow-mattress-colour of
the office-day noon-hour mezzanine
                    that is the sky downtown.

Q: 'The Head of the Horse
        "sees" you say in that poem.
        Was that your vision of
        God, at that period
        in your development?'

Who I was then we
both approach timorously –
or I do, believe me!
But I think, reading the lines,
the person looking *up* like that
was squeezed solid, only a crowd-pressed
mass of herself at shoulder
level, as it were, or at least
nine to noon, and the p.m. still to come
day *in* day *out*   as the saying goes
which pretty well covers everything
or seems to, in *and* out then,
            when it's like that: no heart, no surprises, no
people-scope, no utterances,
no strangeness, no nougat of delight
                    to touch, and worse,
no secret cherished in the
midriff then.

Whom you look up from that to
is Possibility not
God.
    I'd think ...

Q: 'Strong yellow.'

Yes!   Not the clay-blue
with rump and hoof and all and almost
eyelashes, the pupil
fixed on you, on that wall of
fake hunt, fake aristocracy
in this fake Sunday
diningroom I was telling
about ...

Us Artists – Before Public Was, or Grants *or* Can Litter

Condeminstrel copia
the archway read.
Not to go in
would unframe my head.

Inside the court
a fountain dribbled
so I stayed on and
hourly sibylled.

Nobody expected
commerce or coin
each one teaching
his own-bound voisin.

One wore a stilts,
one a daubed top-hat.
Well, among us
we were satisfat.

The chestnut leaves
rotted us under
and you'll find that archway
now a choke of cumber.

Sestina (1964)

Eyes keen, because you licked sticky wood-honey,
Jonathan? You shrug at a rumoured fast
for scared unequipped men. They quail to see
these fierce Philistines milling around in their blood,
earth heaving underfoot, friends' faces hostile
enough to kill first, under the dire bright arc.

From the felt virtue of the holy ark
how should Saul, king of the tribes, extract the honey?
A father, he stands tall, hasty not hostile.
The household that holds Jonathan fast
outshines royalty's luminary, through blood,
as this wild breakfast gives the son to see.

In the printed Word, I, astigmatic, see
your name, in the sacred calorescence an arc-
lamp bright through my carbon generation's blood.
The enemy braces our leaf-stuck stony honey-
combing metropolis. Our young heroes are fast
with a buck. And the holy licks at us all as if hostile.

Is it the host on earth now that makes us all hostile?
Our day too soars, a cliff where the prince could see
the follower doggedly climbing, breathing fast.
Tales puddle down to magic, or moviehouse arc-
hitecture in celluloid: 'Jonathan has a honey,
his at the cliff-top, coy till he risks his blood!'

Samuel's grief was harsh, foreboding the blood.
The priest is no popular leader.   Don't tell us the hostile
megatons hide under that affluent honey
of words. We cover our ears.   We do not see
the mercy in the flood story about the ark
for paired progenitors, though it still hold fast.

The young, sensing aliens all sides these days, fast,
too angry to earn or eat, afraid of blood.
A million candle-per-sq.-inch project the arc
down, on the graph. Fortune and time are hostile.
Most are forlorn. Self-exiled a few see
their land out with the locusts and wild honey.

Who dares any longer break fast, dares be not hostile?
The Son's blood clears a dawning arc – oh see
Him with aghast disciples, sharing the fish, the honey.

Embezzler (Luke 16)

1. His Act

The 'unjust steward'
    called to account
invoked the principle of quid-pro-quo:
a little kindness, scattered in a
mesh of diminished debts and muted
    obligations made a
    stunt-man's safety net.
At least the others' debts didn't seem appalling
    when his own were plain past hope of more
                        stonewalling.

Anyway, who could honourably venture
fairness to Mammon's lord, being his creature?
His shrewdness actually tickled the manager
and – 'good PR' – made the firm feel
taking the loss still worked a general benefit.

The storyteller knew
their world: the rich man and the steward,
customers, sheds, primary industries, the
sea and airways, the
delicate networks of blood, breath's come and
go, the dark lord and the quick
wit too. He knew about people's
nimbleness when caught.

He dares to let the
wisdom of the world
commend that steward's feathering of his nest:
so a closed world of rascals
closes in lord and vassals
with what they choose.

11. A Classic Case?

The truth is,   all we 'have'
is not owned.   How we appropriate
            this goody and that, and pad
            the books, quick to do favours
            from somebody else's coffers!

        O yes   our accounts look good.

            We almost thought that we
            had made it, had it made.

When we're called to account
there's – fleetingly – relief:
we really cannot ever make it good.
But quick, before we're out
on the street,
fiddle those final ledger entries
so made friends may provide from well-stocked pantries.

III. '... wiser than the children of light?'

Taught and furnished richly but in debt
by not living it out
we can be stiff when caught

and duck the blame
and in haste in another's name
on lesser small-claims culprits lower the boom.

Wasting goods in trust
can go so far it cuts
a man completely off his storehouse access.

Yet who could feed
that steward, fired,
except the backdoor beneficiaries of the same affluent lord?

iv. The Wastrel Begins to Hope

But who's really in charge?

The friends he eased
met his necessities
despite his years of waste.

      Brimming hours of days
           and fruit of the sun
      are trusts; also the powers
      in one physique burning, and around him
      in others' energies. All fit
      into a brimming life-ful-ness, an
      everywhere poise of parts in their best places.

To never waste minutes, muscle,
money,
would be to not fail.

Yet, failing, this man still
was not quite wasteful
    employing all he had
for those who would be able to provide:
the story does not call *him* 'good'!

      There has been One who proved trust-
      worthy. He does not waste
      a word. Stripped bare to give, He then
      entrusts, awarded all as His possession.

For the Murderous: The Beginning of Time

Cain brought grain on his forearm
                and a branch with grapes
        to the plain earth
        under the wide sky:
vaguely he offered   to the far-borne light
what the slow days had sweetened.

Abel killed, from his flock.
On the fire he made sacrifice.
Fat-brisk rose smoke and sparks,
and blood darkened the stone place.

        That this was 'better' than that
        kindled in Cain a murderer's heart –
        he was watched over, after; but he kept apart.

In time the paschal lamb
before the slaying did
what has made new the wine
and broken bread.

All Out *or* Oblation

(as defined in 2 Sam. 23: 13–17 and 1 Chron. 11: 17–19)

Where sandstorms blow
and sun blackens and withers, licks up
into empty bright glare
any straggler
            who is exposed
                        being still alive,
there:
    clean   cold   water
        throat-laving
        living
            water.

    Look! – a little group of men:
    sun flashes
    on the water poured from leather pouch
    into a bowl, shining,
        now uplifted.
God.
God.
        Saltwater has etched
        their cheeks, their mouthcorners.

WHAT ARE THEY DOING?

They are crazy. They are
            pouring it
            out.
Sand coats the precious drops and darkens with the life-stain.
                            Earth's
            slow and unspasmodic swallowing is slowly, slowly
                            accomplished.

No. I do not understand,

yet with the centuries still gaze at them
    to learn to expect to
    pour it out

    into desert – to find out what it is.

Dryness and Scorch of Ahab's Evil Rule

Elijah said, this way comes no refreshing, only famine, drought. (1 Kings 17)

Elijah's raven was a bird
of prey, a scavenger.
And yet he was – Elijah heard
it right – God's messenger.

His wafer from no holy fire:
'this grisly flesh – or die'.
Cherith Brook alone was pure
and Cherith too went dry.

Elijah swallowed what the bird
of doom there dangled down
until the desert.   Then the word
came, and he could go on.

A widow had not needed ravens.
Now her one son lay starving.
Elijah begged.   'Well, all I have is
gone, if I risk serving'....

She did.   The boy lived on;
the prophet still endures:
the unfailing meal and oil a sign
to last through centuries.

It consecrates a time
of bony men and doom
lit towards the bread and drink of Him
whose is the final kingdom.

He Couldn't Be Safe (Isaiah 53: 5)

He chose a street
where he wouldn't be safe
and nobody there would save him.

He went to the parties
that were not safe
not saying who, but they knew him.

He went down the road
to the Place of the Skull.
The soldier was there, and the criminal,
and the ones who thought if he didn't have pull
they wouldn't be safe to know him.

He couldn't be safe
and come where we
go, and hide,
and storm, and agree
on everything else if only he
wouldn't show up our artful way
with the light of his simplicity.

No. He couldn't be safe and be
our Saviour.

To Emmaus

'Are you the only stranger in Jerusalem
who has not heard?'
The Risen One wandered their road with them.
Their beclouding had not cleared
and did not lift even from
His word.
He simply came when asked at evening
and broke bread there, a third, with them.
And abruptly they were assured,
beyond all that seeing had suffered
joyful.   They hurried
to those who had not heard.

'The Lord is risen indeed,'
the welcomers cried.

As a Comment on Romans 1: 10

Paul petitioned to go
to Rome 'by any means'
and was led by the centurion
to the Emperor's death-row.

Yet he urged it. He was
glad these new Romans existed.
His wisdom was enlisted as
their ally, to find them his.

It did not save his neck
or probably theirs:
he knew beforehand that when light appears
it must night split   and earth quake.

The Circuit (Phil. 2: 5–11)

The circuit of the Son
in glory falling
not short
and without any clutching after
His Being-in-Light,
but stripping, putting on
the altar-animal form
and livery of Man
 to serve men under orders
 to, into, death,
 trusting the silent Glory
 (though at that instant out of touch) –
  flesh marred, heart
  deliberately benighted
  till the spilt Blood on the criminals' hill
  split earth and Temple veil
  (then all was silent,
  cloth-cased and closed in a stone hole) –
 to prise, till touching with unflickering Breath
He prises even us free:

this circuit celebrates the Father of Lights
who glorifies this Son and all that He
in glory sows
of Light.

The Bible to Be Believed

The word read by the living Word
sculptured its shaper's form.
What happens, means. The meanings are not blurred
by Flood – or fiery atom.

He reads: a Jewish-Egyptian
firstborn, not three years old;
a coal-seared poet-statesman;
an anointed twelve-year-old.

The Word dwells on this word
honing His heart's sword,
ready at knife-edge to declare
holiness, and come clear.

Ancient names, eon-brittled eyes,
within the word, open on mysteries:
the estranged murderer, exiled, hears at last
his kinsman's voice;
the child, confidingly questioning, so close
to the awful ritual knife,
is stilled by another, looking to His Father –
the saving one, not safe.

The Word alive cherishes all:
doves, lambs – or whale –
beyond old rites or emblem burial.
Grapes, bread, and fragrant oil:
all that means, is real
now, only as One wills.

Yes, he was tempted to wash out
in covenanting song
the brand on the dry bone;
he heard the tempter quote
the texts he meant and went embodying.

The Word was moved
too vitally to be entombed
in time.   He has hewn out
of it one crevice-gate.

His final silencing endured
has sealed the living word:
now therefore He is voiceful, to be heard,
free, and of all opening-out the Lord.

Listening

Because I know
the voice of the Word
is to be heard
I know I do not know
even my own cast burden,
or oh, the costly load
of knowing undisturbed.
There is a sword
enters with hearing.   Lord,
who chose being born to die
and died to bring alive
and live to judge
though all in mercy, hear
the word You utter
in me, because I know
the voice.

Light

The stuff of flesh and bone
is given, *datum.* Down
the stick-men, plasticine-
people, clay-lump children, are strewn,
each casting shadow in the eye of day.

Then – listen! – I see
breath of delighting rise from
those stones the sun touches
and hear a snarl of breath
as a mouth sucks air.   And with
shivery sighings – see: they stir
and turn and move, and power
to build, to undermine, is theirs,
is ours.

The stuff, the breath, the power to move even thumbs
and with them, things: *data.*   What is
the harpsweep on the heart for?
What does the constructed power
of speculation reach for?
Each of us casts a shadow in the bewildering day,
                              an own-shaped shadow only.

The light has looked on Light.

He from elsewhere
speaks; he breathes impasse-
crumpled hope even
in us:
that near.

11.

That picture, taken from the
wing window, shows a shadow.

High up, between
the last clouds and the airless
light / dark, any shadow is
– apart from facing sunlessness –
self, upon
self.

Nights have flowed;
tree shadows gather; the sundial
of a horizoning hill in Lethbridge measures the
long grassy afternoon.

Still, freed from swallowing downtown blocks of shadow,
I note self-shadow on
     stone, cement, brick,
relieved; and look to the sunblue.

So, now.

III.

Flying Air Canada over
the foxed spread snowy land,
we look where light is shed
from lucid sky on
waters that mirror light.

The magical reflectors there belie
factory   and fall-out   and run-off effluvia.

Where is the purity then,
except from so
feebly far aloft?
Is it a longing, but to be brought to earth,
an earth so poisoned and yet precious to us?

The source of light is high
above the plane.   The window-passengers
eye those remote bright waters.

Interpreters and spoilers since the four
rivers flowed out of Eden,
men have nonetheless
learned that the Pure can bless
on earth *and* from on high
ineradicably.

From a Public Library Window

The uncoiling, jointed, glass-and-duragloss-
plated, flowing
serpent of traffic will
be stilled.

The seemingly stilled, upthrust
office and apartment towers
and smokestacks
will with the slow
of brickdust-Nineveh's flow,
(and even the basking hills)
sift down and be all through.

The tissue moon
still floating in skylake
and the sunflooding sunfire point –
        swivel of food and drink and sense –
from before Adam, wait
for the once opening of
the Golden Gate.

Only the Unchanging One
is, inexhaustibly, un-done.

The Effortless Point

Three long-distance runners
out for buoyancy
pad by me, leaving the weed tassels a-waggle
and are past the sumach clump and
fleet, into brightness flowing,
they bear along
              lungs
                all rinsed with morning.

For Richard Rolle, swift in the strength of stillness,
flowed light,   and the   out there   flooded
his pulses
leaping these six centuries –
love breathes him so alive.

Moving into sky
or stilled under it
we are in the becoming
moved: let wisdom learn
unnoticing in this.

Oughtiness Ousted

God (being good) has let me know
no good apart from Him.
He, knowing me, yet promised too
all good in His good time.

This light, shone in, wakened a hope
that lives in here-and-now;
strongly the wind in push and sweep
made fresh for all-things-new.

But O, how very soon a gloat
gulped joy: the kernel (whole)
I chaffed to merely *act* and *ought* –
'rightness' uncordial.

But Goodness broke in, as the sea
satins in shoreward sun
washing the clutter wide away:
all my inventeds gone.

Hope

It was a clear bright world
from a shining source.
   Along the way it has been spoiled,
   gross-warted by the cheap and coarse,
     inwardly, worse.

 I'd thunderbolt it down
 to shred in withering smoke
 if that way everything could drown
  in all I've found of dark –
 then to-be-born ones in the gold of dawn
 need never even look.

The shining one looked, and said 'we',
owning one source with us.
That chokes the heart unbearably;
here, where we grope and fuss,
dully we hear, and dully wonder why
we did Him in for this.

'Why you did? No. I chose to come
and knew the way was through
your flesh and blood and doom
of death. I, judge and lover, knew.'

   A death You *chose*?

'First. Yes.'

 Somehow a clear bright world
 wakens at the voice.
 The glory has not filled
 His long appointed place
 but shall, because
 He knows.

Contest

Having in Adam chosen to know
we are sorely honoured in
choosing to know, I know.

We do know what we do.
The second Adam chose to know but
to do otherwise, thus condemning
all but the goodness He
thus declares knowable.

Grimly we concede it, who
would rather do and know,
until as we are known we know.

Into the Vineyard: A Vision

Among the quickening thud of wings,
head borne steadily on past the chokecherries' branches –
ears and nape of neck as formal as
Indian pipestem, or sea-wake of
fresh-turned loam, or wings,
all alike breathed by purpose of wholeness –
he goes, straight as a sunshaft, not
ducking from the angel. He
simply walks on.

The sun burns down on all
who linger and who go.

On Goodbye

The radiant distance, not transparent, remarks
calm trees in evening water,
or remote childhood fields, window-seats, quilts,
on the blank hourlessness the old
stare at and so bless;
this distance seals
both parties to outwardness; it is
itself the poignancy it would leave
to that failed place
where no one is.

Distance, through this time I listen to
you, learning not-being, looking through for
an analogous point in vacancy,
with walls of you and me,
as boundaries, set, that that which is not may be.

Intercession

To leave it in God's keeping
is not to turn aside
from the caring or coping
and not saying it's all right.

Is it to discover
when heart and head
are prayer-held, that the members
are to-be-healed?

He knows His body
here, must be
caught up in and ready
for long-suffering too.

The old saint, because of her
long hours not spent afield
therefore with searching force
waits it out, for us:
wounded, and healed.

As Though

One looks about at the green-hung room of this earth
as though as seed in the soil
still, and about to split
rotting with reaches towards the
inconceivable elsewhere,

knowing no purposing, only
a king of atavistic feelers-out,
as a comber shells,
arched, day after day, to
shatter waveness.

Nevertheless
becomings are then in now;
unbearable unless
suffered:

hope stirs,
not surges.

Backing into Being

Feathers skinned off
but pinions ribpressed in,
I, squeezed in muffling
dark, go narrowing

knowing a point of light.
The day withdrawn-from here
a funereal ointment
seals off anywhere.

(Dark – with day still in sight?
The hole is from a place:
once as a child I foot-
groped back through a crevice

out onto a sheer cliff;
the sweating fingers slipped;
falling towards rock and surf
my I unslept

memorably.)   Let go
till forced I may not.   Crawl
back to false everyday
is inadmissible.

(That bird – whom I would
love as my neighbour – comes
from the place the tensile cat
twitches, and will pounce?)

I shrink back into dark
towards a threshold of fear,
beak gaping and quills barked
all for hope's lively danger.

The place remembered, and the here distress
still pinpoint for us final skyfulness.

Scar-face

Scarred – beyond what plastic surgery
could do, or where
no surgeon was when blasted
in the wilds or
                on a side road –

he prows his life through
the street's flow and wash
of others' looks.

His face is a good
face, looking-out-from.

City Park in July

Walking on thistling grass
in sandals stepping in the crisp
drought-barnacled grass-crust,
I see a city gardener smoke
through weed-crumbs with his mower. But
the park pine is still glossy:
its roots stab down, and deep
in, find the winter run-off still.
                        I swallow
depth. My thirst would fill
dark reservoirs against a
desiccating brightness.

Hope rises very deep.

The Engineer and the Asparagus

Asparagus, once established, bustles
it grows so vehemently,
cone by cone nosing out towards
those (unseen) garbled acres and the sun's
tusks of flaming.

A person – as the dentist meticulously,
       silverly, nicks him out, under
       fluorescence, in a dead air, with the gutters
       tinily gurgling –

a person
compacts his growth, shells over
sore decay spots, and retracts,
       coil upon twanging coil.

Put down the dental floss, the number nine iron,
the gear knob, the wire-clippers, the periscope and fins.
Just put down, for a minute, the obsolete
  stencil-stylus, the ink-pad stamp, the farmyard
                gas pump feed-line.

Down tools.   And in
abashed intervals
let us abound
asparagus-like
(straight up through the driveway concrete!)

Neighbours?

At the carstop
in the tarpots' fume
weltered, you walked
past, stranger, like a found
manganese nodule – concentrate
of mortal meaning on the
seafloor of the city's
daytime din.
The streetcar jolted on.

'What speaks?'   The stranger's
face and walk compel
awareness still.

To contemplate is an
indulgence, distancing
a self, an object.
To mine the meaning of
a found identity
will be given only to
recovered innocence.

'Then contain,
content to wait till Then.'

To Not Know When It Is the Worst Is Worst

Berries in brambles, loose, or pressed
hammocky by feeding bears:
fresh-water springs, resins, some roots:
fish baked in coals of smarting-sweet shore fires:

w e   c a n   r e m e m b e r

       though habit-tranced we steer
       the jumbled shopping-cart through supermarket
                                  aisles.

W e   k n o w   o f   w o r s e.   But

    I'd rather outstare
    thirstlessness, where the sub-Sahara shrivels
    and grasslands sift under the glaring skies,
        than have had doctrine I could leave

        as the storybook-picture cook at last abandons
        recipes,   bowls,   and blades
              stove,   spatulas,
        in a foodless,
                garbageless,
                      always sunny and clean

      forever meaningless
           kitchen.

Where sunlight quietly delights
in wild fruits and clear water –
or where the dry wind serves
as only scavenger:

in both alike, food is
untheoretical.
Known.   Or unknown.

81

Emmanuel

'With us' in this pain
though His is the morning
of all promise, the morning
of only hope,

to be done with it all, there,
now, and choose nonetheless
this place:

in that   in today   in pain
He makes Love plain.

Needy

I.

In part, who isn't
    miserly with his need –
    or needled by it –
    or debonair
    as though it were not there –
    or, at best, genuinely free
        to need yet never be
        needy?

II.

'The poor are always being
inspected: by the
    Fire Department, for litter, oily rags, those
    lamp-cords from the washing-machine to
    the hall ceiling socket, etc.;
        by the
    "worker" with new forms
    to be written on;
        by the
    mission visitor "to invite
    you to the children's pageant";
somebody even inspects
to check on whether it's true you keep chickens and goats!'

III.

Home after a day of calls
she absent-mindedly pulls
the curtains first
and then acknowledges a thirst:
everything has run out
again tonight.

We the Poor Who Are Always With Us

The cumbering hungry
and the uncaring ill
become too many
try as we will.

Try on and on, still?
In fury, fly
out, smash shards? (And quail
at tomorrow's new supply,
and fail anew to find and smash the why?)

It is not hopeless.
One can crawling move
too there, still free to love
past use, where none survive.

And there is reason in
the hope that then can shine
when other hope is none.

Psalm 80: 1 – 'Thou that dwellest between the cherubim, shine forth!'

In autumn dark comes early,
the wind goes to the bone,
the crowds are very busy
and a person feels alone.

You know, Lord, You know us
out in the dark and cold –
and never planned to leave us out
although shut out of old.

The windows of the glory
were open, and You knew
Your power was for outpouring
in time to make this new.

We didn't know You, Jesus.
You came out in the night
and poked around the side streets
to bring us to Your light.

We waited where the wind blew
and knifed You in the rain.
Yet You still know who's scared and cold
and doesn't dare complain.

Some You have given food and warmth
now can go back out to
be with You in the darkness,
vagrants, focused on You –

until all the windows
of the Kingdom shine
and we can all be very sure
You wanted every one.

Bless us, Lord of Heaven,
Bless us, Mary's child,
and keep our courage high with You
through steep and storm and wild.

We Are Not Poor, Not Rich

Rita tends to see
the earth vanish she stands on
just as she lifts each foot
(you keep on going on)
but seeing Vivian with wheels
   and on a road prepared
presumes her terms translate
into undoggedness innate,
i.e., going by vehicle – not on foot.

Yet Vivian, driving, knows
whirling uncertainties
and simply keeps on, as she goes,
as Rita does.

And I can barely snatch
my foot free when the soppy sand
goes slack
and fills in my old track.
Yet looking up from this Despond, I note
a pilgrim firm of foot
and think he's on a better road
               – and think then wrong.

Speeding by the unmoving is
for each alike a known
blessedness not our own.
And each, in that, goes on.

Transients

The affluent city shaves the turfs
(laid one sun-streamy March morning)
by tractor-mower, tenders them chlorinated
and fluoridated rain from
sunken spigots through a wib-wab spiderly
sprinkler.
            And in July a high-rise
enterprising developer, to
excavate, uproots
the lawnstuff, uncouples the subsurface
aqueduction system.   The city
waits   alert   even with all that
dirt blowing in its August eyes:
             ready to spread another quilt, in squares
             somewhat rough and ravelled, from
             truckload stores of good fat cakes of grass.

The city ('it' I called us),
fluent, unruffled by February sop-root
or Labour Day cloth-and-sticks,
lights up at night.
It lays and trims and turfs up and
replenishes and hardens in vacant lots and
parking lots.   We are forever
doing, done-to.

             The grass grows
             strongly, it has twitchgrass in
             it too, ready even
             to shag the tracks and blocks
             if we fall
             silent or
             simply let be.

To a Pioneer in Canadian Studies;
and to All in Such Pedantry

'Give me the camp-out times'
said the prospector.
'Then when the floor gets dirty you move on
upstream and build your fire
on the clean rock, and make you up a
springy cedar mattress....'

Sweeping those old floors
he left (after the blizzards and the buzzards) for
traces of transient life
is work.   In your steel vertical files
old sweet woodsmoke aromas and
springwater bubbling out and beargrease
so cherished, vanish.
Blinkered graduate students peer
with you in the green light
through memory mesh. You are
breathing – O, carefully, untouching
Canada in the cocoon there, as it were.

Serving and preserving, you together
may yet perpetuate
the thankless pioneer,
and when the campsite is a clutter
move on, to the clean ancient sunwhite rock.

Speleologist

The seller of irrelevant sweets,
souvenirs, and tickets to the caves,
in a board booth
in an upland pasture
on a September Sunday (gold
and grey above-ground;
bat-coloured, earthworm-coloured,
oozing, below)

> is not a seller in a booth
> really, not a
> scientist, excavator, engineer,
> adventurer, entrepreneur
> amongst tourists, really –

he is the naked hiding poignant face
of an earthwork, himself, of centuries,
inevitably the one to
spy out a place of rushing
underground rivers and to break
through, wade in, raft blindly down,
wriggle up soapy chimneys niched for nothingness
    in tinkling total dark,
knowing all rock-webbed vaults,
                arches, hollownesses,
as if beyond the reach of light.

> For he is there,
> himself, though in his odd board booth
> in the September sunlight dozing over
tickets, or (hazily) pop-frigidaire,
cash register.

A Blurt on Grey

I hear far off the unseen:
in 1940, war
from Canada became
all ear-shell and eye-glaze.

Now, in the small-wars-decades
under the newly rainwashed roof
lying by open windows
I hear far off the unseen
wedding party's horns
within a Saturday of garish and drift.

I remember a 1940 wedding
not far from Montreal, in June:
all alone, in
a deep-green hedged field, sunken
in the steeped lingering light;
the rocky outcrop and bunched cedars
breathed grey and stillness. And
there, well I knew
how this place framed the tank and flare,
the bloody set-up, booming oceans away.

To hear far off the unseen
can make a here of there
without absolving one from having been
summoned to home or being
enlisted here at home.

Absolute

Right here on earth
I've known One Person who would
see me in the worst there is

at the core of it – see me
    e.g. the mocker making a frail rabbi
    hop on the Warsaw pavement   yes   at the worst
                                  would see me
    lazing and lording it over him or e.g. nobody
                                making me do it
        willing to hop on the pavement
        fearful nobody really
           making me
    or e.g. would see me
      turning away from both in
        order
      to be beautifully alone –

one Person who would
nevertheless care
enough to to be past
tears   *lacrimae* would never be past minding that
                I'd broken the good
                    lost the best
                    gone past the most I'd ever ask or hope for.

It transfixes,   finding
Someone who means risking
tireless loss
in a real world   e.g.

      along the lake road with evening pale already
          and nowhere to turn off:
             right here on earth.

Embattled Deliverance

These thinning woods and dry
meadows and scored bluff,
guerrilla nor refugee
find mutually enough

to thatch, let alone nourish
their elusive corps:
eyes flicker at twig-touch and
too near at night earth seeps.

Thump and faint dab of fire
from the great powerfuls
is ungermane; a far
din defines silences.

Come as it may, the clinch
finds ones, gashed (shin or forearm)
but longing for the once
winning, the lustral corpus.

Christ, bright of hope, be
there, calm with your tapers,
in ceremonial care of
our tremulous ardour's.

Poem on the Astronauts in Apollo XIII's Near-Disaster

(written April 17–18, 1970, for the newspaper)

Friday a.m.

        Intrepid the three are who
        out past the blue
        float
        powerless almost, without
        washed air, become almost
        morsels of earth-lost dust.

        The crippled spacecraft will
        bring them back home, if all
        earth-generated beams
        of intelligent response
        to all that may occur still
        keep them criss-crossed, can forestall
        disasters, one by one.

Friday p.m.

        They are safe down,
        the representative men
        in a representative planet, not left alone
        when the air and power were very nearly gone.

Saturday

        We in our millions cruise along
        in the encapsuling blue
        not sure why we belong
        on earthship's crew,
        all at some instant scared
        to find ourselves aboard
        and not sure what to do
        for safety or for rescue.

A Man could launch the lot
    and did so.
John the beloved ('all things were made
    by Him') says this is true.
And our hearts and stomachs for this are
                           thought
spaceworthy, valued at
more than the ride, too.
What of the where and why?
Let easy analogues die
on our lips – we float, not 'fly',
keeping check on the fading air and power
                               supply.

Air-burn, the ocean, divers, nets and decks,
    quarantine, doctors, complex
        debriefing days
are not the NOW that grips all our energies
as knowing, both the dark possibilities
and the bright, grows.

Kohoutek

The comet
among us sun and planets
I saw with naked eye, i.e.
nothing between my ice-
    keening
    tear-washed
    seeing
    from earth-mound (here) to
ocean-deep navy-blue out-there (there).

        In the traffic-flow
        a frozen lump
        from a jolting fender
        spins meteor-black
        towards the midwinter bus stop where I stand
        under the tall curved night.

Veering weird-brightness
from somewhere else:
we solar-system people flinch
        as at a doom-sign,
and find you cryptic
      from far unlanguaged precincts
        soundlessly hollowing past us.

My tongue, palate, lips, teeth, life's breath,
pronounce 'comet', call off
as told
how many million miles away
I with the naked eye still-standing see
you, it –
of quite another orbit.

Christmas Approaches, Highway 401

Seed of snow
    on cement, ditch-rut, rink-steel, salted where
    grass straws thinly scrape against lowering
    daydark in the rise of the earth-crust there
    (and beyond, the scavenging birds
           flitter and skim)
is particle
    unto earth's thirsting,
    spring rain,
    wellspring.
    Roadwork, earthwork, pits in hillsides,
    desolation, abandoned roadside shacks
    and dwelt in,
    unkilned pottery broken and strawed about,
    minibrick people-palaces,
    coming and going always
    by day all lump and ache
is sown tonight with the beauty
    of light and moving lights, light travelling, light
    shining from beyond farthestness.

Slow Advent

In silver candy seeds
worked into shortbreads,
a manger and
pentangle star
        – oh, how to utter?
The all-enabling Infant 'lulled'
in romance verses,
and plaster, painted, amidst stagehands'
hay and incense
        – oh, how to express
                even the animal *richesse?*
Stitched in wool
on kindergarten paper and
in electrical street-dangles, aglow,
the emblems
        – oh, I too desecrate
         the holy hush
            to trumpet:

    joy in the newborn, so
    far, His
    coming, so
    small to all my anticipating sense of
    majesty, yet

    indomitably coming:
    the flint-set-faced
    ready-for-gallows One,
    on, on, into glory, and His
    place of my being to be
    His   as will every
    place
    be.

Christmas: Becoming

The Breath – flower-gentle, in,
is Word of power, out:
creating that invisible City, and
mountain,   forest,   sea,
tundra,   ore-vein,   light.
            I knew it was forever, for I was young.

The world one day
cracked.
Faces all went grey,
cords, slack.
            I lived towards the mortal Friday for-
                              ever till caught
                              in this.

A stranger flesh
of only son of man
torn and entombed, but raised
timeless, then
            – the eyes turning to look up blur before him –

is still the Christmas presence,
flower-frail, approachable:
the timeless Father does not leave
us broken, in our trouble.

            Even citied, at sea, shop-bound,
                  the *here* is veined
                  in light.

Midsummer Christmas

Blind under dazzle, aggrieved, held together by
knacks and knuckles, our
warfulness waits.

Don't come here, Jesus!
No.
What You must know here
who can, unless to the obliteration of
the flower-light of Beyond,
                              the far, still hope?

And yet,
oh light us epiphany in humid July!

Behind the open casements and French windows,
in the pantry
in the parlour and window-seat, in
cupboards, velvet
cutlery cases, everywhere
is preparation for
festivity.

He comes.
He left His name, letting it be
given to parents, shepherds, temple habitués,
the village, friends, courts,
executioners, the
Ghost-jubilant; and now
to July's children it is given.

Waking and Sleeping: Christmas

A frontier woman felt
awe, the same awe, she said,
at childbirth and a dying bed.
Yes, said the doctor,
tremblings that reach your heart.

     Too few
     have to know these enough
     and specialties and techniques grow
     that ward exposure off.

Isaac went confidently up the slopes
in Abraham's shadow, unaware
until the sacrificer's knife flashed up:
then the branched ram was there.

     We carol as our earth
     swings some to outer nightward
     and sunfloods the Antipodes (sing forth
     we both, in seasons sundered!)

The newborn in his mortal fairness
moved those shepherds, and the Asian savants,
from other, usual, bent and stress,
to helpless, awestruck jubilance.

But hard on the manger vigil
came Herod's massacre – like
the Pharaoh's once – and Rachel's
heart then broke.

Outside, the hills, sea, sky
wait – mild. And welling
from past the horizoning why
a new light flows, is filling:

coming far down, away
from the enduring Father,

the Child, alone, sets out upon His way
to the cursed tree, His altar.

People tremble and yearn;
our dark hearts thud
in case that light will burn
and wake the dead.

Then

The leopard and the kid
  are smoothness (fierce)
  and softness (gentle)
    and will lie down together.
Then, storm and salt and largeness, known, in time,
    will be within the wholly pure,
        the unimaginable!

    Then, the fair blue
    will not be star-extinguishing;
    and one cascading meadowlark
    an all-where will not deafen;
    acute, prefiguring moments
    of our leaf-flickered day
      will lose none of their poignancy
        when they are caught up, Then, in the
        all-things-upgathering bliss.

    Here, then, prophetically,
    in the strange peace of the outcast
    on manger hay
    lies a real baby:

        all-cherishing, the unsourced,
        the never fully celebrated
        wellspring of That Day.

Creative Hour

The universe our colouring-book:
    'Child, fill it in'? –
or a waxy page to scribbling shade in, and make
streaky pictures come plain?

The outlines vanish.
The tentative image fails.
Chalks smear, all the paint spills,
creation crumples and curls.

I'm down to bone and awe.
Where is this then –
no clock, no lunch, no law?

What is learned, I unlearn:
and hunt out an art school
that may require a model;
or contribute a membership as an art patron;
or, anticipating the generations unborn,
set about knowing what the subjects mean
and how artists have done.

The evasive 'maker'-metaphor,
thank God, under the power
of our real common lot
leads stumbling back to what it promised to evade.

There is no one reviewed, no viewer,
no one of us not creature;
we're apparently at work.   But nothing is made
except by the only unpretentious, Jesus Christ, the Lord.

Research

'Do your children have nightmares?'
said the doctor to the parents.
                    (The wallowing monster;
                    the hairless purple face;
                    an elbow out from under the bed;
                    and that turned-to-marble chase....)
'Yes.
Signals of sickness,
or punishments they dread,
or something they have seen that preys
on their minds till they understand.'

The doctor asked the children
whether they thought
adults had nightmares.
                    (when that chalk-blunt thing walks
                    across the green evening – with a
                                        broken elbow-hinge,
                        not gumless, not
                    darker in breath among the airs that
                                                    stir
                    along the floor of evening, but
                        nudging –
                    in sick distaste, people
                    swing doors against the sky
                    and sealed in lit boxes ask
                    no questions. The doorknob doesn't
                                            twist again.
                    Picturing that bland pace,
                        the forearm jolting loose,
                        makes night's palate dry.
                    The caves along that cliff are
                    left to the gannets.)

'No. They go about
bright rooms till late.

They know where
they are.'

All sleep. And discover
they're child and forebear,
both, together.

From Age to Age: Found Poem

The steady streetcar windows
pass the window squares
of the department stores:
this is Toronto, queen
city, Queen Street. Next come
the flashing, flowering, high-crest-
low-fall-and-level-shine
City Hall fountains

and in the back of the streetcar here
rises the voice of the morning
                    WAH-TEE!
as in the morning day
when Adam names the animals.

Then the light sharpens;
suddenly shaman di-
dactic, he cries:
                    LOOKIT the *Wa*tee mommy!

Stop succeeds stop.
The day flows over him.
He communes here, absorbed, confiding,
at one:
          ('oo ... oh ... watee!')

Is it all past?
He murmurs still ('hmm ... hm') grounding
elation and surprise.
Storm clouds, dove-grey,
eclipse the blue and gold.

West farther still
every windowed car will be
threaded through
the far lake light and the reflective low
waters of Grenadier Pond.

Wonder: A Street-car Sketch

Judgment as well as mercy:
  that these could fuse
    is staggering.

  A little girl at an open window
  blown wildly, safe beside
  her mother (on the aisle) is flooded by
  colour, motion, glass-shine, sidewalk marvels
  blowing and jewelling in.
  All alerted, she turns
  unable to bear alone the pour of wonder.

  The strong young mother (is she fighting sleep?)
  steady in the bucking and swaying car
  has one arm up, stiff, palm over the eyes.

  The little girl cries 'peek aboo!' and
  yanks at the awkward elbow
  baring (oh, she is weeping)
  the wet and swollen flesh
  eyeless as a fair and quiet moon
  suddenly at crash-down range.

  Briefly they are together.
  Then the hand closes down.
  But the little one's face does not crumple
  or burrow; with a flickering smile
  she snuggles confidently
  back, absorbed with the now
  limited wonder still.

Child in Subway: Sketch

A whirr of dry air
   cement crumbs cinders newspaper scraps
      grits the eyelashes from
         the people-bobbled stairs down to the subway.

A child, stumbling at the steepness
and the hurrying hurrying,
hangs on, then boldly tread-skims
the steps on his parents' arm-ends,
heading eagerly towards
brake-scream, train-rush,
door-clatter, plastic glare and tunnel-plunge,

     wherever his day's lifetime may
     go in its faithful unpredictability.

Bereaved

The children's voices
      all red and blue and green in the
      queer April dimness –
      just as in Ur, at dusk, under the walls –

      are a barbarous tongue,   lost on
      that unmirroring, immured,
      that thumping thing,
          the heavy adult heart.

The children's voices are
the immemorial chorus.

No Time ⫷

The Jo Poems

So Many Years Later:
Preface

On a stormy morning, sun-tinge and tumult of cloud release the
sombre earth tones of autumn trees. The last green, the grass verge,
glows under that overcast.

Death looks very different when viewed from the end of life, death
of contemporaries: quiet, a kind of fulfilment. I reflect, for example, on
my mother – She lived 102 years and eight months. Only this morning
do I suddenly remember one of her contented adjustments – to washing
her hands and face in bed: the thoroughness around the ears that her
muscles remembered from the days before bath-tubs or running water,
when as a young woman she enjoyed her sponge-bath. Such a subject
heavy, oppressive? Surely not.

But why go on to the Jo Poem sequence? The abrupt cataclysm
upon word of the untimely death of bp Nichol leaves everything altered,
and so did Jo's death, for me, when we were both young still. At first
comes the obsessive rehearsing of the final terrible days – everybody will
have their own equivalents – and then, gradually, cherished times and
occasions gleaming out three-dimensionally, not a remembering, not
turning the pages of an old photograph album, but a refreshed shining
out of the person clear now of time, and unforgettable.

Josephine Grimshaw (née Siggins) grew up on a small street in
Toronto (off Dufferin-Davenport if you know the city) and came to
university on a scholarship. We met early in our first year. When she
told me the name of the 'honours course' in which she was registered, I
heard for the first time her characteristic laugh, a mingling of innocent
delight in the absurd and sardonic awareness. 'Social and Philosophical
Studies,' she said, and laughed. The Depression was still unresolved by
enlistments and war industries, and Jo had experienced urban poverty,
indelibly. She met her husband while waitressing during a summer
break, and he too was proudly 'blue collar' by background and by
choice, though he was a journalist as well; and Jo's choice, given her
firm purpose, led through graduate studies and the bureaucracies in
both Ottawa and Toronto. Her laugh supplied a running commentary
on these settings, as it had on campus pretensions. At lunch-hour,
during school or, later, meeting from our various jobs, Jo's eyes would
dance while she regaled us with some event of her morning, or her eyes

would be fixed on the others while she listened; she never looked at her plate, just groped at intervals. When a predictable spill resulted, she would laugh that same derisive-delighted laugh, putting herself in perspective as she did the stuffy old world.

We had an unplanned desolate gathering after the funeral, and one person who had worked in the civil service with Jo gave us a glimpse of her work. (I met him on that one occasion only and do not recall his name.) He was a statistician under Jo's direction working up the data required by some Ontario Deputy Minister to support legislation on minimum wage rates for the province. Whether the outcome was the 1960 law, or the 1963 amending legislation, I do not know. Jo died in 1967.

Their section was working to an assigned deadline. Overtime was increasingly involved, and cheerfully accepted on the whole, because they all knew that any delay with the supporting documents could be used as an excuse for stalling on legislative action. One afternoon the Deputy paid a visit to their section. He and Jo conferred, and the others went on with their work. But on his way out he turned and said to Jo, now in a voice they would all hear, 'I am sorry that it's earlier than the deadline we had set, but we will need your analyses tomorrow to have the time we need if we are to include the legislation in this Session.'

Then, Jo's friend reports, she picked up the large glass government-issue ashtray from a nearby desk and, as she hurled it to smash against the wall, she said, 'We will have everything completed for you tomorrow.' And the whole section rose and cheered, knowing it probably meant no let-up for a night and most of the day ahead. 'And we made it,' he said, 'and so did the Legislature, in that Session.'

What did Jo look like at that time? Sun-streaked, corn-coloured hair, those flashing (or dancing) blue eyes, a face agreeable in spite of a long jaw and slightly protruding front teeth – orthodontics had been out of reach when she was little. She wore her skirts long (perhaps not bothering to shorten them), and 'heels', usually walking briskly with a heavy briefcase in her hand. She was thin but vigorous, and her whole bearing was resolute.

The valour of her public service I wish I could properly celebrate – her field (labour economics) is foreign territory to me. The sunniness of her friendships, with all sorts of us, I do know; and her joy in their rambunctious dog Frodo; and her stubborn persistence with piano lessons as a beginner in her thirties; her equanimity in icy flats during low-income periods or in the comfortable house they later owned, and their hospitality, I remember; and the family's support for one another and their respect for their own and other people's privacy.

Why delay so long with 'the Jo-poems'? At first, to give perspective, i.e., was the initial version just therapeutic writing, an effort to relieve my own grief? If not, what was the source of uneasiness every time I reconsidered it? Had Jo's death uprooted a whole tangle of vegetation that only time could sort out?

In the end, that initial version, most of it, is here, tangle and all.

Full daylight among the trees and buildings outside the window now, a busy world in a new day, far out beyond the time of Jo's life here. But parallel griefs go on. And by now there seems to me something to be openly commemorated.

⇦

Taking sides against destructiveness
brings on the very evil of destructiveness
unless it is clear that
no two persons
will or should
entirely agree,

i.e.

one must so take sides.

I.

Thank God, somebody spoke plainly, but humanly.

The skills of statisticians
mastered, lead through

The knowledge of administrative law
compassed, leads through

The questionnaires, the tallying,
the scrupulous data, all lead through

to the step beyond quantity,
beyond measurables,
beyond concepts,

out where theory is
challenged by the existence
of persons

     for whom (through
statistics, law, data, wearying
detail, unwearying work)
dignity, the structures of dignity
may yet be
          provided.

God help us if we can't remember this.

II.

One winter-kitchen place we were, glassed in, under, together:
glass-frames were painted green. The chairs were
painted. Some had curtain-
material cushions on.
The snow-light mushed across from the
          outstretched west. Family and guest, we ate
          a family meal. Then time expanded,
          time to be there.
You wore a cast and
hobbled (newly moved in).
You spoke disconsolately of the city left
behind: 'maroon plush
reception halls, glazed office warrens,
savagely cold, ice-antlering, wire tangled.'
The 'work' was done
but it turned out to be
in-process model-of-work, instead of
honest work. (On Salem Avenue where you
grew up, Jo, awareness comes baldly.)

After good hours, the coffee pot
glued up the oilcloth.
Our cups went cold. Ashtrays overflowed.

III.

Today, July 18, 1967,
one troubled night beyond
the time-freeze:
      Jo there, locked in, flat down,
      overwhelmed (alone) with
      waves of total pain – the
      dog shut up in the house lopes between
      the suffering and the glass-panelled
      front door, lopes, hopes to be
      helpful, is
      intent; whimpers....

Husband (from work) and son
coming almost as soon as the city ambulance to the
hospital. But someone else
knew? and long, so long
they did not know.

      So many
      into Emergency, the
      waiting
      room.

A handful of nurses and record-keepers and
one or two doctors. People
sharing dimes to make their calls and
telling each his own story and
helping each other find the washrooms and
apprehensive:
('if you have your own doctor' it
'helps'). So few to help too many
hurt, to answer so
many anxious.
The youthful doctor knows two things:
his human sense of what one being feels,

even the other, the not-himself;
his range of competence, the immediate basis
for making rush decisions on
three 'cases' at once (and hundreds 'outside'
'waiting for beds').
One clouds the other; he feels he must deny
his feeling.

> For the young doctor this denial seems
> essential to keeping a social trust
> (as he works on in his own
> corner).

For Jimmy and David, at the moment,
terror polarizes (the
utter need to trust
and angry consternation when a doctor,
    seeing, denies).
(The old father on the telephone
weeping – 'I only keep praying all the time' –
to One who once shone forth
against gravecloths and clay.)

> Yet my heart chokes on earth.
> My questions choke me.
> Who could discard any who cry
> 'I can't believe' – an only mortal truth
> spoken in death's presence,
> airless in its silence.

The body of death is judged now, will not stay:
    newness will come, at one touch,
        aliveness; – but
there's worse than nothing, any other way.

Coming to that hour
meant choosing to endure
these groanings, too, so choosing, rather than
letting a grave-cloth-and-clay body be
no worse than simple death's, eternally –
if that Cup had been tossed into the grass, to lie
abandoned, and rabbi and friends just slipped away.
But choosing so to die
means, here, and there, through love
life for good in its full power
of resolute splendour.

Teeth set, taking that dare,
facing (among the rest) the questions we
stare at till, slowly, the old horizons
    fill with shining, overspill:
        faith, hope, love, are one;
        faith is not alone.
        One is not alone.

Word spreads. Concern
rises. Helplessness
paralyses. Here is the warm-hearted
loving well-loved friend whose
heart has been open, though
seared by disorientations, danger,
dullness, toothache, the shock of
cultures, and of denials, keeping clear
a beauty almost revealed.

At work. A green
branch and a brick
wall. A telephone call.

Tears welling wholly for one who 'just
   heard', quickening to
      the too much:
'It begins to seem
as if it is unlucky, knowing *me!*'
   (Where is the power
   to bear, to be
   fully released, fully
   available?)

Myself, in the odd march
of these developments: very
practical, very
sensible, very
up and down in emotions. And
evasive, looking not quite at
their suffering, all
three of them
and her father's alone at home,
dimly aware of the
strange pressure of a Presence, of a
prince of this brute, bald,
groan-choked, clammy
time, or of all
in time and out.
Fear. Panic fear.
                'Help us
      in this thine agony
      again.'

            Lake blue through
            blowing lilacs
            deepens skybloom

            One dead Lombardy
            brooms up among

greenness fresh-billowing
(bottle-green ditch and
dandelion: foreground)

The day lifts up
(from full-bosomed loveliness)
our railroad sadness,
tearless,

from behind windowglass.

Josephine, sorely beloved of God,
that day instead of trying to
tell, I found you dying.
Out in an almost capsized ship, the Lord
'rebuked' the storm.
The storm that swamped your life
so suddenly
somehow, surely, too, he
rebuked. Calmness
unshakable, came perhaps
when you lay still, only asked
for Frodo, that gallumphing animal
who'd led me to your bed
through the locked door
and then lay near, beseechingly,
fixing us with devoted, steady eyes
until the ambulance came.

Abraham knew by faith
that the boy Isaac mattered –
yes, to all *three* of them –
and so could totally risk
submitting. And
all three, finally, mattered.

My friend is dead.
She did much good
first in her family   also in
her friendships and not least in
tough-minded steps towards
protection for the most exposed,
e.g. the night-shift dishwashers etc.
  who come and go within a week
  too ill   too far forgotten
  to care that 'no work' is
  also 'the worst', or maybe
  simply not able to recall
  which all night spot it was
  they should be turning up tonight....

She cried both 'Thank God' on
the day of the attack
when help arrived, and,
in the throes, her head
rolling, through set teeth
'O Christ, O Jesus Christ' –
as I had heard her
over our thirty-one years about this earth
together, in
uncontrollable laughter, in
anger, in
outraged impatience with
unjustness, in
all the bright patches of her
staggering sense of the absurd.

My friend is dead.
Her parents, counting on their only child
say 'Joey's – gone!' as though
she'd skipped again, as

in the black thirties she was 'gone' to
marry, game in the teeth
of every kind of –
    cash   and in-law   and
    Chapel-vs-Catholic
                opposition.

Only now we learn
why she and Jimmy so often
walked hand in hand. He
broke his foot, the day before she died,
stumbing at a curb, and
refused crutches – 'I couldn't
see far enough to
put them down safely' . . . .
    My Lord, in horrible need I
    turn to the Book, and see
    sin and death, life in thee
    only, and cannot see,
    O living Word, I cannot see to see.

I love this friend we've lost.
And the two-dimensional good
that was all I knew
                apart so long from you,
I cannot now dishonour, or belie.

But the truth brooks no denying.
There is a word, are words,
that do not lie.

My friend is dead.

    The Book speaks of a Body:
    all that we know of wisdom, art,

insight, perception, released only by
some marvellous touch within the cells
of other parts – from the alerting
    head
    all-seeing, hearing, knowing,
    remembering, receiving.
Surely this is beyond
analogy, beyond any blunt
ending or comprehending.

A singled body died
the death most shameful,
most grisly, long-drawn-out,
exposed, with
two 'other' offenders
also under the emptiness of sky.
A glory nonetheless
shepherded the lacerated clay
from beyond stone to
move and speak, on the roads,
on the shore sands, in where
we are.

My friend is dead.

Already goodness enhances memories.
A goodward life flows strongly
for all our implicit otherness.
    Can one cell be inflamed perhaps, pain-radiating
    from pinch or twist, whatever
    the Evil could devise,
    but in the body still
    active, touched to will?
Long suffering is an ongoing   loving
unto health ('how long,
        O Lord')?

My friend is dead.

It is hard, knowing
on beyond your heart,
so slowly, and so little,
          only that
reverence for persons is what
love, truly, can be.

  A place of wrangling roots
  moves the young to petal forth
  nitrogen-breathers on shrunk curly shores with a
  pulse other than
  our lung-cleared veins' and arteries' –

  listening, I almost hear.

  The air flows, lighted and strange, through
  my nostrils, is
  my present
  but now   not   our
  present.

V.

On the doorsill of her death, afraid,
that clear bright Saturday, I prayed
and around four there stirred
pain-brilliant joy, holy accord.
Confident in my will, I waited for
a hospital report, sure of a healthward
turn. They said.
  'Condition poor.' I soared
  away from what they said....

But couldn't there have entered
her hectic solitude an
angelic poured-out joy
visible only as new tiredness?

I do not know. The lift
was real, for me.
And yet   I'm not the one
to tidy up a sum as though a
life of intricate bright and dark
and the huge mystery
of loving work, evasions, tactics,
home emergencies, and
sudden sickness, and dying shut off
by the sense-dimming ice-floes
where no one could follow
that I can know –
as though this, in my friend,
or in the lives 'lost' from any 'view'
that truly knows,
as though for them some passages were not part
of the all including.

The river of Life carves out
    its uttermost channels
(here 'hardening', there 'yielding').
YES. BUT.
These human words burst out
and will.

VI.

Daily and lifelong, Josephine,
you gave voice to the mute
hoping the deaf would hear, who all
too easily, in affluent times,
relegated the poor to a category
(the 'residual poverty' of efficient,
ah, and political, theory).

ɷɷɷɷɷɷɷɷɷɷ

Having

Sir, you have nothing
    the woman said
Nothing to dip into water
    or carry water in

On the empty-handed earth
the snow stars blot and fur and dwell
    roughing eyelashes of winter grass
    and on the open gaze touching, muffling.
On the snow the slow, rich sun, in time
Seeds   roots   coolness
    through a new sundeep season.

The heart listens.

'You have a cup
when I have nothing.
Both must be
for still refreshing overflowing new-day
    joy to be.'

ɷɷɷɷɷɷɷɷɷɷ

The tulips were cherry red.
  Now splayed out they are unable to
    breathe out the light that falls on them.

          ᴨᴂᴨᴂᴨᴂᴨᴂᴨᴂᴨᴂᴨᴂ

Boys toss sticks
aloft   where spring
lit chestnut candles. Now their swollen wicks
lack not even polishing.

Reaping is rough
on field-mice in
the bloodied stubble. Grain is enough
to garner since that only nourishes man.

Dying is fall
or leaf, or day.
A body sculptures desuetude,
outguttering. And yet, it will,
in time, know everlasting awe.

          ᴨᴂᴨᴂᴨᴂᴨᴂᴨᴂᴨᴂᴨᴂ

Sky and earth seem to strike each other.

VII. Pruning

Deciduous scented
truck basket, fragrant
branch-loppings in
full leaf, branch springing and
toppling upon branch, twigs
shedding green and wood crumbs on the
curb-line from the truck's trailing
as it starts up at a signal.

Were these branches
diseased? No.
The leaves are squeaking with juices.
Was their tree or were
their trees then
hurt? Can its (or their)
sap flow and diffuse to invisible leaves?
Some trees are trimmed
for buildings or wires, and some
for sturdiness?

Pruning. The
new air
washes in, almost
visual, with
the beautiful, bitter green.

VIII.

Wheat and blue sky;
a sloping hill
golden and blue
and still:
     your colours, Jo,
     your clarity.

The sunny snow
of January
your birthday time,
bright, with winter birds
trampling the snow, tilting the limb
of puff-laden tree, and scared
by a quick laugh, a slam
of a door – away!
     your window, Jo.

There need not be, there are
no words for
what is clear.

Now our hearts gather
dear recollections
wordlessly
together.

IX.

Only all looking to the core
of life's forever Fire
– no more centrifugally –
can any be.

x.

Once there was a court
doomed, and a scheming
truth-anointed, cold
assassin, doomed to succeed
the by then suffocated king.*

It is told that a long look passed
between the speaker of truth and
the one who would soon be a murderer.
The anointer spoke words only
of (truthful) hope for
the victim.

But then he broke down.
The murderer, startled at this weeping,
asked 'Why?' – did he want it named
in advance? It was
focused, surely, on him?

The speaker of truth was racked
by his people's coming suffering
under the heartlessness of the oppressor.
But he spoke, he submitted in truth
to the Purposer of
what was to be,
weeping, bowed at His knee, not suppliant but
in ever-deepening love knowing
he was not in control,
could not be, would not want to
foreknow more than he must.
He clung to love as the end and so
could honour both truth, and trust.

---

* 2 Kings 8: 8 ff.

The Hid, Here

Big birds fly past the window
trailing string or vines
out in the big blue.

Big trees become designs
of delicate floral tracery
in golden green.

The Milky Way
end over end like a football
lobs, towards that still
unreachable elsewhere
that is hid within bud and nest-stuff and bright air
where the big birds flew
past the now waiting window.

Denatured Nature

The little toothpaste-foaming waves
have wilted one wasp on the wet sand.
Last winter's snowfence sags. The beach
is drifted with washboiler
jetsam; and   tossed scraps
of paper, one old shoe, give evidence of
party strays who flitted
here, before spring.

The fussing water
wads the wasp's wool,
pulping this too but
salvaging nothing.

Patience

Still, still, the trees in morning thaw,
sealed still against steel cold
and ragged on the windward sides (the conifers)
let wilted-petal light
tip-touch every needle, the least twig,
motionless.

They are prepared
for onslaught when the obliterating
blasts sweep in again.

Meanwhile they dwell
thus, now.

And they are ready
even for spring, to swell
sing break spiral shimmer
transform,
when that becomes the
inconceivable now.

Dark Afternoon

The sun is white,
snowblear all stained, and
radiostore music
parlours this grimy salt-besplattered
sidewalk.

The time is furtive, seeming late,
unfurnitured, fit for hunched
non-householders, and for ghosts of a
pre-city, one-day day.

Compromised – and Fighting:
1988 as through the Reign of Ahab

Building, celebrating, feasts,
selective hearing of appeals
(with many too nervous to appeal),
persons accounted for, and beasts,
a desert-locust whirr
of life: no edge, all blur.
Am I subject to Ahab? I concur?

    Whining when pushed, and left aside
    in valorous protected pride,
    indignant – while I hide.

The clover-delicate light withers. Soiled
rags of cloud smear down.
Blunt moths glue to the dingy pane.

    By one act in the clear
    I might declare
    one phase of truth
    and yet still play for truce....

It rains, upon the just and the unjust:
snowsoak and sloughs of April merging
until worked furrows become slop,
a muck, where seed will rot.

Fertility cultists, note
how lush begins to bloat
with bluegreen brilliance – but nothing for food.

    Moralist. Scold. Blue ruiner.
    Begin to learn to be less rude.
    Conserve the drastic judgments for export.

Sunscald on cliffs
sunblinding
water-glitter mirage
salt scurf
sleeves of sand
sand hems, and sheets of sand
(cliff-silt, so sand-powdery) sunwhite scarfing
shifted and shell-mingled and swept
so shadow-shaled even a fly's foot skids.
Crumbs cast shadows.

Here, also, angels minister.

Anti-War *or* That We May Not Lose Loss

On valleyfloors under the sea
crews of old sailing ships sidle.

Whose is the cliff-path, whose the sun-bald doorstep
signalling still, 'Here he will be
no more'? Whose? – and not being sure –
makes desolate ocean's floor.

Cities have vaporized. Somewhere in slots
or stalls we have parked the bolts
for the blue to sizzle the fat
off the world, or all of it desiccate.

Grieve for the bracken, the honeycombs set in the
   orchards,
grieve for otter and chipmunk, and those who yet on the
   verge are
trusting grown-ups for food and future,
jumpy, weedy, clouded
already by the foreboded,
or unafraid and dwarfed by that.

So many losses sing
in the ears as though unsung.

Still, steady days roof over
Jill, Alexandra, Christopher.
Clicketing cities speak their
various tongues, delphineal poplars
tremble with morning light
or shine in evening. Every single one:
Go on! Go on, to know
in time even the least

blessing – to cherish in want on earth
fhe dignity of one significant death.

Horseless City on a Rainy Thursday

Seething and smoking, the rain breathes
earth and wet board smells, juniper-berry smells,
dog's fur; O, and the pale wet
smell of a shin stripped on the cherry bark
in a near fall. This day
dwindles us, only absurdly. See
the usual street-and-corridor range as though
a ladybug rambled along
the buggy-shaft in an old shed,
sensing around its small self
context and whole conveyance –
slant and athwart and boxed and
contrived, though horseless now –
in a remoteness, a somewhere-once, abandoned.

Watery sun
appears. Ladybug tentatively
unfolds a wing.
Still the ditched farmyard steams
here, in the almost empty shining streets
with their curbs foaming.

Cloudburst

Earth (meadows and rock
gardens, perforating cities,
crepe sea-skin, people, slag mounds,
highway access ramps)

Earth (i.e. all within the
circle of sky)

suffers, today, the rain.

Plip plip then
(crack!) it's boiling everywhere.

It singles itself into
slow droplets on car windows.
The forehead feels its skyward touch.

Rainworms emerge, deep waters
under the earth are nurtured
and, gradually, the roving clouds again.

Earth suffers the first large splats, the rush, the pelting,
    the beautiful withdrawing,
variously receiving, mirroring, waiting
for the long wind, for evening sun.

Detroit … Chicago … 8 a.m. … Platform 5

We queue in long young shadows
for the 8:00 o'clock bus
to the far country.
It finally shows
up at 8:30.

One, when he delays
has good cause:
outrageous care, still hopeful promise.

Does he delay?
>   the timetable is not posted.
>   The depot is where each is engaged till then.

Why have we less, then, trusted
  this perfectly punctual
     perfectly considerate
        perfectly timed coming

than – at 8:27 – we still unquestioningly expected
the 8:00 a.m. bus to the far country?

Meditation on the Opening of the Fourth Gospel

Un-tense-able Being: spoken
for our understanding,
speaking forth the 'natural world' –
'that', we (who are part of it)
say, 'we can know.'

Even in this baffling darkness
Light has kept shining?
(where?   where?   then are we blind?).
But Truth is radiantly here,
Being, giving us to Become:
            a new unfathomable genesis.

Come? in flesh and blood?
Seen? as another part
of the 'natural world' his word
flung open, for the maybe imperiller,
in what to us was the
Beginning?

The unknown, the unrecognized, the
invisibly glorious
hid in our reality
till the truly real
lays all bare.
The unresisting,
then, most, speaks
love. We fear
that most.

Just Left *or* The Night Margaret Laurence Died

Bare branches studded once with jewelled birds
Someone inexorably plunders
One by one till an
Impoverished wintry sky from hill to
Darkening hill reveals
Untreasured tree-spikes, almost only
(One bunched bird left
His eye aglimmer there).

Waiting, dim
Loneliness, place of
That withdrawing vision –
More than the well of light from
The first far planet –
Fill, fills, fills, fills.

Mutable mortal night
Blinds mortal day
Still to changelessness.

The perched, askew,
Will ruffle still as the day-ocean
Lips in and foams towards flood of
All emptiness exposed.

Standing Centuries

In remote Ur of the Chaldees
a primitive man utterly alone
is struck, a coal shedding stars
deep as space has grown.

In elegant brightness, linen and stone
finality, Egypt rose
mirage-clear under the blue when
famine was stalked by the Jew's

deep prisonrock-born eyes.
His people – near that throne
and in time slaves – by force
were (skeleton or steel) withdrawn.

Crumbling waves behind, a dune-
carved sill on nothingness
except sandstorms and silences to hone
down an arrowing purpose

fire-cruel on cluttering cities,
petal-queer on the clean
stem of the water-freshened place:
ununderstood life flowed on.

Judgment and corruption
cone up, tumble aside, release
the kingly gold and ivory, the stone
lifting its awful grease-smudge and incense.

From the shepherd-kings's loins
through refugee years, mean
resignation, compromise,
essential fires burned down

to an outcast's child born
in the cot of the beasts.
(Shepherds heard silver horns
from remotely royal stars).

That life against our own
makes much make no sense.
Who doesn't hear wild John?
Yet even his repentance

won't let even him in
to unlatch the sandals of the sourceman.
'Not worthy' he says. He can
only wait till that one

himself comes, puts on
the towel, looses the sandal thongs,
kneeling. He began,

being of the Alone,
the singing that, from the farthest down,
lingers and will resound.

Radical Hope

The blessing *(la blessure)* of growth
given in the broken Root,
                    First-Fruit from death
as from the death we laboured for so long
now gives life worth.

Earth is now opened too
to astronomical warmth, to cultivation
as rain and secret earthworm tunnellings
prepare the way,

thawing now root-force,
proving that strange power
hid in a seed for growth.

For Jessie MacPherson: A Tribute; a Portrait

A welling-up out of the earth
as brownly twilight brings on
night in the prairies,
surround of richly human pain:
not your own, not
ours, not –
even in the bedrock you insisted on –
known or discoverable ...

That slow horizon-wide
curve, that engulfing
caused austere excellence to so
deliberately *soar:*
music – as only rises from
such silences.

Silent Night in Canada in 1848

The night, a winter moon's, was distinctively
still.
The farmers near the gorge
heard it emerge
large and unreal, and lit their lamps to pull
on boots and sheepskins and go look.
They saw Niagara-no-Falls: moony rock
with here and there a slack
curbed puddle in the moonshine,
table-paving and threshold of cataract
as actual, still, stone.

In England tallow snowlight fingers
warmed branches on the hedge;
here a son, there a husband
(among the Sikhs, some, some fighting the Trekkers
between the Orange and the Vaal)
are a broad earth-curve far from home.

Erie is wide and shallow and windswung
in a black-bushed stump-rough nowhere.
News is hard come by here
and who's to care
on the escarpment in March weather?

The moon floats round, reflecting
1848's Europe in turmoil – and
in Chile the intellectuals too
infected with revolt.

A violent gale had
jammed the ice
from Erie's floes to form
a wedged wall, locking in a vise
Niagara's sluice.

The moon floats over David Livingstone,
enjungled, planning his next walk
    out across Kalahari,
over multiple campaign pennants, over
the cradle of – eyes buttoned shut in
                sleep – one Paul Gauguin.

The farmers stare at the rock, rock at the moon.

Now while it snows we linger
stunned by the roar of the Falls
and the river unrolls, unrolls.

Processions. Triumph. Progress. Celebration.

At roadside, spectators
gnaw olives, all eyes, as
the Inquisition leads its 'victim' who is
also gnawing olives (old friend,
you saw, remembered, that)
before the hood was
lowered, and the rest;
sweat shone on his cheekbones.

Next showing: a blaze of bands, then
the ominous drum-beat, shoals of parallel shins
trampling, glazed
eyes, so that children are
puzzled, distanced, prance
alongside. The elders look
locked in an odd paralysis.

We see by satellite, screened,
the war matériel crunch along
tractored, mounted on massive dollies,
peopleless, cash-cold (there, or
bunkered, along with a
'control' panel connecting
people to buttons to the matériel to
death, not as usual).

Celebration? That
waits for the end of war,
and not by winning 'ours'
and leaving 'theirs' to be
resumed in time. All, we and they
together, gather
this once, holding our breath,

awed, watching,
         waiting, all
spectators, all participants
       at last.

April

Dark like a handful of cool grey silk.
Clocks strike the hour. Out in the clear-gleaming sky
a robin's song, silence unravelling.

The trees with tremulous-aching fingers
shaping the quiet airflow.

Sick-faint dark
limp in the arms of the infinite.

Sparrows

Do tiny ruins, glimpsed triangles of parquet,
tempt stopover, or the shepherd's purse a-wag
or skeletal milk-weed? The frail millions
flit hither
blown like the wrack of hurricanes
along the barrel-ribs of sky.
Some will be off again
to tundra summer and the chill
promise of it and of death.

No bird-memorial commemorates
the prince of sparrows, in this their park
although our king in bronze
is here. The sparrows
in suet season, and through
carbon monoxide summer till
autumn's enlarged outdoors,
quick in their public middle age
keep hidden delicate and final things.

Only whiskered cats and the
hidden lover see their stillness, and
the devotees of cats.

Seeing So Little

In the tents of day,
under night's canopy so
long – why
do I still not know you,
sparrow?

    hop   hop
    flit   swing on wire
    hop   flurry in dust:
    quick take-off,
    tailfeathers snooting threat....

But can you step?
In the parades of years,
burnt-orange summer,
whistling fall,
and the scouring colourless
seasons of cold,
why have I never seen you walk?
Toes yes, legs yes,
but knees?

I do not want to face the fact that
loving watching you, over
ranges of long time, I
learn so little – yet too much
to 'look you up'.

Orders of Trees

In France, woodlots
form tidy colonnades
with canopies, in season.

Young orchards and
Christmas-tree farms in Canada
go dwarfly grenadiering and
form columns, wheel,
for passing trains.

Farm bush is clumped, then clear
under the beech-trees, thinning
out to white pine.

Burnt-over land or
logged-out land
shows modestly harmonious proportions
of new life in one brief
lifetime.

Forests existed before us
ancient and vast.
Now we have made our planet
bare-faced.

The woodlots, orchards, farms and groves
make arithmetical comment.
Not contrite, boasting no improvement, we
nonetheless persist.

For a Con Artist, Who Had Given
the Worker a False Address

This morning, another con
I guess. Nobody known
that name   this address.
Snow   sun aflame   children
fawn dogs dreambound   green
leafmat under snow ...
but   nobody I know
though I am nobody to
hide from, God knows.
The wide blue
morning is alert   lovely   wordless
with me: waiting.

To knock next door is
neighbourly. This sunny little block
right on the cartracks feels
friendly. Here there dwell
a mother, boys, potted violet,
tortoiseshell cat. She tells
me finally about her cataracts
and how next door the woman
died months ago, and there
was nobody that name there
since, or before of course.

Walking away
into the wide of day
I wonder why
threads fray so under a
blueness and shine. My
foolishness podgy with joy
contemplates the absurd

credibility of the
shouted-by-ranges-of-angels-down-to-earth
reality   that embraces
this street and her not on this street but somewhere,
indulged, a little, at least
for now.

For Milton Acorn

Tufty and bristling and, yes,
covertly nest-downy in spiky branches,
for the hurt of wing or not yet
free to range.

I'm sorry, Milton.

You loudly speak for the dumb still
using words culled from
the jewel-box and the strewn
back-yard of derelict motels, etc.

Still, the
sawed-cardboard voice.

It surprised me when a long rant once
faltered into sweetness at one pink cloud in a
sad evening sky. You spoke of Shelley and
took wing then, quoting by the yard....

I'm sorry, Milton. Not an apology.
Sorry, with you, that one by one awareness
arouses anger, and you get scrapped
into the safest stereotypes:
'character'; in some lingos 'poet' too.
You don't care though, snorting and seeking out
lotus-petals, white water, and bright skies.

All You Need Is a Screwdriver!

Frustration finds no anodynes
as hours of darkness rise and fall;
the 'should have dones', the 'could have beens'
have me in thrall.

Sleepless? from creativity
in me the spoiler. (Ah, when corn,
wine, creatures, suns, all came to be,
seventh-day Joy was born.)

     A diagram a plastic sac
     of bolts and screws and little pegs
     a box of sides and front and back
     and, yes, four legs.

     The picture all completed glows.
     You need your own tools too? just one.
     And as adrenaline now flows:
     it WILL be done.

     Right the first time! ? Well, 'up' is down.
     What has been joined can come asunder.
     Reverse, rescrew: the process known,
     now there's no blunder.

     Empty box two, spread out the plan,
     begin assembling with a song.
     With so much practice now, how can
     this one go wrong?

     It could. It did. 'This one' had glue
     as well as pegs and so on. Haste
     made waste: again the wrong way to,
     and bonded fast.

Another day another try?
Pervasive smell and flaking smear
of glue – and solvent. Let it dry
and call an engineer.

Well, I am more than construct. No
diagram lays out how, or can say who.
Spoiler and spoiled betimes? I anyhow
can yet be made anew.

Meeknesses

an examination room, to the examiner,
    whether medical or academic,
    whether with stretcher and gowned patient or
    young scholars flushed intent submissive,
presents pathos.

The one open to alien
evaluation now is past
risking, given over
to an assessor.
    Waiting on his pronouncement
    tomorrows stand uneasily blank.
To the examiner
the pathos is his
imputed power, too.

On Peruvian plateaus or in the
mountain valleys of Irian Jaya
people with symptoms live, or die.
And wisdom there listens, fingertip sure, alert
to the bright waterfalls, and ponders
the antecedent hidden springs.

Night's End

In sleety dark
the bouquet'd trees
are held deep, under earth.

Slow flambeaux.

Green life doused still by the
pale rainswollen clouds.

Grass now watercress-green through melting ice.

Unlidded, skylit world.

When We Hear a Witness Give Evidence

Who heard the angels' song?
Those on the night-shift. Maybe
the animals. Not mother and baby,
not Joseph, innkeeper, wise men,
not the soldiers or Herod. Not Elizabeth's John.

The glory (that *once*) was clear
of those in waiting on him who now
was clothed with only our here.
Heaven knew this was the hour.
The Father gave Himself over.
A few heard the angels shine, stricken with wonder.

Joblessness now, or night-shift,
nine-to-five or in Chronic
Care waiting it out:
we like to quibble, we hear
and are faintly afraid, are sore.
No, there's no angel-song
tonight. But when someone tells it, something,
a Presence, may briefly shine
showing heaven again,
                    and open.

Timing

In pallid winter oaks
only rustled still.
Now, woodenly they bulk
leafless where all the air is flower-frilled
(lilac and almond-blossom). Why
are only oaks so black in the bright sky?
Even in spring's rich overflow
pupae are curled in clay;
the winds that straw the lovely blue
are somewhat radioactive, too.
'Earth felt the wound.'* Ambiguous nature stings
our sameness eyes: her songs
somewhere, somehow, take wing.

———————

*Milton, *Paradise Lost*

City Birds

Pigeons are pedestrians
chiefly, therefore becoming threatened.
Seagulls take
over in the park.
Around the bench where bird-
charity is dispensed
they squawk like highway casualties,
and rise: sky litter.

And in the November wind they,
tilting against the sullen overcast,
shine white, in a
flash, before,
stray dots, they
remotely scatter.

My Mother's Death

1. The End of Chronic Care and Other Kinds of Unpersonhood

Institutionalized love
is not   in the end
especially
love.

The end seems always alone.

Love was there   before ... is
person   waiting.

The Epistles on slavery
mean this: I mean, service as
dead-ended in what's done.
The lovely Presence waits for
some hint, some beckoning, in
a place squared off and framed
by 'principles', where
'siding with life' is a   slogan.

He,   waiting,   is.

And those He was before, is/i.e. would be/ with,
eat out their hearts alone
waiting, some in
even-here-unfrustratable
love.

11. Call and Recall

The *I AM* only, here and there
and then, and now – and on –
abides. The near
light of the Lamb, there all, never goes down.

Late afternoon through the west window (closed)
beats on the beds, on immobilized
patients in Chronic Care numb in the glare.

Low sun-rays wince on face on face
in the prone populace of this
staring-eyed place.
Curtains? As inaccessible as outer space.

Silent, motionless, gone
too far to reach, each one
feels, thinks, recalls, but deep in, far far down.

Blank as scarred downtown playhouse walls
these persons cover for
remembering: curtain calls,
storms of response, appropriate – now, but there.

Long before institutional care
my grandfather grew old. We were
children spellbound in his atmosphere.

His inner-lit wondering eyes
helped convey angels; stories of Abraham
abide; memories rise
cairn after cairn over the years: the *I AM*
defined by stones in time.

That inner light of the Lamb
is near still, even here.

iii. Suspense

Age is the belfry.
Tongue of the bell my heart.
Wind wakens rumours* but
an unweighted rope still swings
and shivers only, earthward.
Wide is the light.
Darkness too may waken
the clangour, sounding out
through the circles of heaven,
    but not where hearing here
    is stunned in final deafness.

---

* The 'rumours' deepen breathing:
  of summer grasses, straw hats,
  wild roses, rain-wet
  boards of the corncrib threshold,
  and grandfather's sweet linen …

IV. Hospital Death

Dark. All alone and dying,
two hours, and no one there.
But the flags of dawn were flying.
The chandeliers of prayer
seem sure behind cold temples or
the cavernous mouth even.

It is remote – that heaven
comforters evoke,
but your last sleep is given
to One I know awake.

v. It All Runs Together *or* My Sisters, O, My Brothers

(thoughts on the days following news
of yet another mine disaster in South Africa)

'The vital signs are good.'
I didn't want to leave.
Before daybreak you died
while I slept on, and live.

> How clear and bright, that day!
> Everything echoed, rang; then
> the viewless orchestra
> stopped at the tapped baton.

Leaving you, then, alone,
you only minded, then,
if touch then had not gone
for good.   I tease my brain
for sense to this distress.
Wanting to hold your life
to the last ebb? and yes,
share, where none can who live?

> Rock thin soil grass mat
> cement   an old machine
> walls   doors   cages and gate
> constitute the Between
>
> for pithead families here.
> (Rescue teams go below.)
> Grip, heart, upon like fear
> with theirs, and weep, and know.

The one I left, those these await
and cannot see:
they, now, are open-eyed with night, to us
unknown, radically.

VI. Place: Given

Snowcrusts and crystals
outside the glass
make snowcaulked skylight of
the hothouse roof, suncold
and bright out there, pastelled
in here with the sepia smell of
peat moss, and small sepalled
living things misted and nesting.

Waterpipe sounds.
Far thud of pot on boards.
Tinkle of icemelt there beyond.

(Lingering too long? ...)

Back at the entrydoor and shed,
outside, it's night:
glimmer of farm lights, wind
whitening briefly. And
before we turn to go

we find we walk –
as though hairspun, but among
such cameo-quiet strangers –
quietly deeper
through greenhouse to where leafy
distances open out,
past trellis, orchard arches:
shimmering, wonderfully
all we'd awaited.
Not way, now – only
now.

Known

After the crash we scan
passenger lists – eyes dart
along, down, till at last we can
relax: this horror was not to the heart.

An 'act of God', that tidal wave
or flood – or the lightning-bolt
that caused this crash? We have
His word, yes. He has all, controlled.

Oh, but His eyes are on
the passenger list too;
every mourning child tonight's well-known;
their dead He, nearest, knew.
In charge – and letting us be – but not apart:
for Him this horror is real, and to the heart.

Our horizons stop at those we know
so we can bear it;
His, not at what we know,
compassing our sheer-edge-of-nothing panic
and more; He though in peace and power, knows pain
for time and space, Whom these cannot contain.

In the Hour

In the hour of sorrow
remembering that
  still evening sky, the
  tall tall treetrunks
enlarges the place of sorrow
for breathing.

     Chill is the beauty
     of bunched seedheads on stiff stems
     touched, touched, touched
     by the light silhouetting solitary
     hedge-seasoned evening wind.

The words of this still speaking
quicken a prepared,
preparing, known,
neverseen heartland where
thankfulness is longing and
longing blessedness.

Winter Looses Winds

The untidy rooms of late childhood
are now ceramic seas
though living gannets cry there still,
settling, rising.

Through clean windows, twice a year,
the outer space eyes innercupboard corners.
Once only in a week otherwise, we
water plants, dust, wash windowsills
so that these squares and rectangles of space
may, meanwhile, unobtrusively, contain
living.

Now old age comes, with
tactics to (slowly) outwit
chaos: what's on the shelf? when
was the last laundry-day?
etcetera? Or with
containment given only to
feral light and darkness
if need be, so that,
inbetween, time may be living,
unpredictably rich,
an order, even in chaos.

Coming Back

Coming back from travels
must feel like this:
elbow-room enough
where you know roughly what's
expected, for how much,
though not quite what's approved;
and where the other people
not part of a transaction
vanish into habit
like peaceable brothers three fields over
resolved into the angelus
the forefathers brought here
in a cracked frame, or like
the implausible blonde on the
service-station's red-and-yellow calendar
on the Trans-Canada Highway
in the long wind.

Ineradicable Promise

When frost comes out of the ground
fragrant with rain and root
in softening hump and ditch,
all new, all sun-embrowned,
the is seems what it ought.

Necessity's seasonal.

The slowly yielding earth
harrow will jag, and plough welt out
till winter contours level.

Still, slowly, more and more is known
of sun, and rain.

O that the farmer heart
were served by the computer-channelled
currency-funnelled packaged and marketable
fabrications where
we scud and skulk, puzzled
by static, loosed to veer
towards lunacy,
because we know the need
but neither seed nor season.

No metaphor for cities under tillage?

O wet, wild, city-scouring March
you smell of soil and stem-wet
here (park triangle, back yard, vacant lot).

Pocket and patch it may be, but still, here
is wherewithal to receive.

Sumptuous Mortality

Children's veranda in the
lowbreathed summer twilight:
'if I should die before I wake' lingers
erosive   engraving

O   not alone   'my soul to take'.
The sweetjuice hay of nightbreath
smothers in luxury. Who doesn't
burrow into being
deaf to not-life for

sleep, a time of sleep.
A handkerchief of waiting daylight blown
in esperance: enough.

Focusing

Given is all there is and
all is
there is
given here and
who is roomy enough for all to get in all given

forgiven and forgiving and given
giving in and
being given there

all is
here

give

Riddle

How can we 'give' who only all receive?
Just as we know who only first believe.

Early Morning (Peopleless) Park

An ornament-coloured hound
prances among autumn's
quivering tassels – morning and mist
in swaths, bright-dangled, tapestry
his lissome zigzags.

The paw pads on the grass-mat
are felt, the pads, now, cushion-whispering
pressing softly and swiftly where
sungold is storied,
                          roomed down,
this rich only as touched now.

Migrant Impulses

Leave this?
    as the Scandinavian tribesman
    fled from the ice, who found
    fire, and the equator – or
    failed to find, among the sleety root-
            ridges stumbling?

Swim the updraught of air   dotty
as birds, mysteriously
instructed migrants?

No 'as' has knowledge of
this force who
desolates and awes and strives –
      not epochal,
      not seasonal,
only: once. Now.

Winds whip the tree.

We twitter and flip
but not in the thinning branches
who have left forms known as trees
      forever. We are
          left to the aloning power
    who gathers us   now
(tossed, tossing)
      I sit in this tree.
    We twitter and flip.
The gloaming draws near.

The sky-valve lets in a
      pallor and chill,
      leaf and stem seal,
      soil is unthirsting.

And others gather.

The flocking, the high homing
in jetstream, strange ice-crudded
light-absorbed ways:

something of that we sense,
        none of it know –
        no rest, no place.

        The summer power was thriving.

Now it draws out
        to a new power, radiant,
            fearsome, for
                flight, far coursing.

To Someone in That Boardroom

Inflooding, dark swirls over
tinkertoy town, not drowning
the light where nightly cleaners clean
or, one floor higher, light
where a committee sits –

so late?
Tired to your wool sox, sir?
Eyes gritty with paper encounters?
Listen, then:

there is a throb, outside,
a hyacinth-core, impacted, under
the rolling wind and night.

In Sultry Weather

I wade on through the exhalation
of the other other
this morning, through the
Name only, not
floundering down.

Beyond the clamminess and this
place of unplasma'd leafage
propped on dim illth and left
in daytime's waiting-room
   there are valleys and shores
   of more or less possibility.

It is the going on (not
   storm and relief, or an escape
   to a wind-clean shore, or a warm sweetgrass knoll)
that surprises, daylong.

The other-longing is enough.

The Sussex Mews

A fawn kitten, with the eyes and eye-rims
of a hayfever victim, intervened
between plantain and back-stoop foot-scraper.
The sounding ocean of the air
blanched the far reaches of the steep green trees
to mirror an invisible surf. The wires
sang to the purple sky. And from the harness shop
came a long sigh of musty shadow.

These afternoon occurrences converged
on children, quarrelling.
The abandoned one turned his face slowly
into the first hurtling raindrops.

And an hour later, watching the welts blurring
the darkgreen windowpane, a child would stand
in timeless exile: from the sky
that served the sun as residence; from the warm
sweet breath of air by the board fence at noon.

                    Supper would be like
lonely Noah's, with his sons,
but without hope!

People Who Endure

Some people who endure terrible things
become terrible, are
selved, yes
then thinged, lumped together, then
earthed.
Earth goes slowly
down (as Noah remembered but said water).

Raining and levelling, clear
eyes only, the unlidded only.

There is for Noah who
trusted, a rainbow:
who built, who dared the lonely deeps,
who woke,
a sun again, and sons.

Conglomerate Space *or* Shop and Sup

There is a mall
under a high-rise tower
that is itself a people-channel or
chute, to the mall
   (which if you saw in small
   would swirl with bubble-people
   around and up and down
   themselves a coloured globe-full
   on display plugged in).

The individual
bobbles along alone
although unusual
clusters occur; and then
the thin-din echoes with a new sinister
sound: a voice, far-hail,
hermetic (O, unrule!).

You even slot your fill
with plastic, styrofoam,
and papered picnic morsel
which, crouched on arborite and chrome,
furtively you channel to the internal
enzymes' emporium.

Yes, under almost every high-rise tower
there is a mall
and still awhile
the lonely storm and sunshaft pour
immensity out there and over all.

When Did the Billboard Clamour on Our
Early Motorways Die Down?

The painted bus-stop pole
is not *colour*.

Behold the trees: their tender
young green
candles the purity of this May morning;
and in behind a patient
grey-auburn rack of branches, although
leafless, is today
lustrous.

Out of our boxes, powders, vats
come signals only.

Colour stills, rather.

Crowd Corralling

Hard rain.
the bean-mash smell.
leaky tin-brim spill.
grass-soak:

birds clotted in big trees.
Cotton people in go-holes:

uncontrollable   beautiful
sheepdogging skypower!

Going to Work

Dog is asleep on the mat.
  The glassdoor is burning
  with morning. You can
    smell fungus and fire
    out there, only to look.

Deal with
your cowlick.

River margin is apple-egg green,
the sun bowling wild past the poplars
and veering left and up aslant
forever.

Coat unbuttoned, eyes weeping,
I sail in sun.

Withstanding

No village store, no gleaning
from a wilderness leaning
off into slab and sky.
And wind and sun and the dread way
hone every body.
Miracle-tinting crazy
hope promises
sustenance – some time.

> No bread from heaven is given
> the fasting one
> who will provision
> his own.

Or follow the green way
out of the glutinous sun-moil.
A 'country estate' deep under swaying
branches offers some refuge from the whirl,
fortifies those who care
to press on, briefly baffles then clears the eyes.
High altitudes shine in the thinning air
from here: we glorify
what, from there, flattens to shops and shacks
and railroad-valleys. Speeding and drifting at once
means nobody copes with the tombstone
tilt (the iron frost found
it alone, in winter alone, and shifted its ground).

> He who in all things worshipped
> always only one
> was therefore with him
> one, always.

From the necropolis follow the tour guide,
smelling sun on the camera casing, following
the striding crusader of an earlier invasion – on still
towards the manger site.

En route somehow lost from the tour
try to follow the book
where cloves and chrysanthemum fade for
'xalapan' ('sand by the water').
Plunge? for the sun?
Patience. Patience.

    Not putting his Lord to the test
    was his command
    and the evil one, to resist,
    left awhile then.

Walking Home, Scarborough

Midafternoon
the sun is white
and all earth's winter wool is
bleared and stained and
radiostore music throbs
tempering sidewalk grime and roadslung spatter.
Sky tinges, dimly then suffuses
and far fresh snow upon spoiled
snow falls thickly, furring that man's eyelashes
and felting footsteps. Even tires
ease their slapdash, begin to feel their way.

Albania Imagined

See the shine from tufted top here
to the pale carved distance over
(delicately, step delicately).

A town thrusts up on the steep of rock.
Every peak and cranny and nook
is lit in the small warm evening – sheer
slabs of shadow and sheets of clear
and casement secrets making the mountainside
multiple and quick and miraculous.

A bubble of music escapes into the empty
zigzag streets, it swims out, darts,
trembles, and is snatched
into the craters of the night below.

Stillness. Till, again, on the mountainside,
tenantless morning's doors swing wide.

Constancy

'Things change,' said someone once
when discomposed to meet
a 'ghost' who called (the pounce
too sudden to defeat).

The ought-to's multiply
and want-to's get blurred in;
harder to justify
they can become uncertain.

Then the have-to's will mean
pressures on the unchanged.
The claims that intervene
no open choice arranged.

Well, intervene they do
like time which makes its haul
without regard. And who
but wants, each in his turn, that large unchangeable?

Future

Yes, the light is pale this day:
lake-light lost in pallor,
buildings without shadow
in watery morning light.
But one triangle of grass leaps out,
vividly green, so that the
silver and saffron and cinnamon
branches, sky-root-spreading,
wait, under the morning.
Had we not seen a springtime
could we imagine leafing?
the surf of wind along the summer treetops?

Patience towards the unknown
sea-light makes only us human
creatures oddly nervous, even where there
breathes an early green, and bulb-spikes show
by the south wall.

Under incomprehension, awe, nothing we can
account for, we nonetheless know
a forceful current:
joy inexpressible.

Paraphrase of Ephesians 2: 1–6

Us, the walking dead,
he has made alive;
by the Saviour, God
lifts us in his love.

Once we stirred instead
at the rebel's prod,
hungry, overfed,
hunting, hunted, bored.

Now His power is here –
though awhile our earth
thrives from holy fear:
the real utters forth.

Levellers

This scarred paved lot has
people places, fifty in all;
white paint defines each of the
paid rectangles.

From here to glossy shopping
is as sewer to penthouse,
set sideways.

O city, city, here and everywhere,
things function to confuse all place,
to dispose – 'mark' or 'colleague'.

Persons can be tricked
to act, though other-wise, to
purpose at least alternate
distorting. Mark and colleague
occupy people places too,
with or without white-paint-assigned
(paid for) provision.

When there is no more call for ruth
either one may be known, as
both.

The Fix

Trees with their toes in
water, spectral, spines
up into watery skies: they still
their air.
     Sorrowful,
those who have let water
be, without run-off, waver,
taken by surprise by earth's slow tilt
until the low land, filled,
stands here, as if at a confusing distance.
Apple-sound evidence
speaks of large plans – hill,
hidden ravine, littoral
and inner continent; and world
in its starred ball-bearings, oiled
with light; the energy is clean and
never uncertain
about limits.
     Old age
rooted in new swamp
sifts the uncertain twilight. Wan sedge
wavers towards the horizon.

Toronto Tourist Tours Toronto

These were seen today:

the sandbox in the daycare yard;
chickenfeathers plastered to the crate-slats and
crates stacked on the littered walkway;
sick smell of streetcar varnish;
a sooted brick warehouse;
tarpots fuming at a curb
and the air overtop obscenely glandy like the
Fat Woman *grande pleine*
turning, turning away.
A demure 'residential district'; there
on Main St. (not so named) a
dairybar, its girls waiting like
Swedish loaves, and its
window display fly-speckled;
in a narrow unused garage
a hand lawn mower waiting to be oiled.

The streetlights have come on.

Corporate Obsolescence:
A Sad Poem in a Sad Summer

The tractor factory once
aproned in streetside grass
inspired long city blocks with
hum and bricked-in shiny glass.
It was given to tootings and
merry gliffs of steam,
and swarmed as the shifts shifted.

Now jolting past
in the bad years
from the hot streetcar windows, see:
old railroad grit, strawed weeds,
boarded-up windows – some
slant-broken in to shadow.
Nobody walks along that stretch.

People live near, across and up
in streets that somehow show
too the hard times.

There they are! People.
Outside a false-bright 'Bowlerama':
crammed almost on the gritty sidewalk is
some 'sidewalk-café' – furniture
(without the parasols); they hoist
tinned drinks from a Coinamatic.
How jaunty, how
almost persuasive.

The streetcar colours are as
glittering-fake as their
café's. Neither
quite gets us there.

Edging Up on the Writing

The fellow in the library who said
he was 'researching a
poem': you just
feel he is likely no great shakes.

    How to learn, and
let shape-taking, in and from,
occur
        seeing one's
        complicity in all other
        molecular chains human and other and
        of 'learning'?

The thing which to talk
as from above it (i.e. the
talker able to manoeuvre it and
other things)
    is positionally to be
    missing it

and to talk of it
as from below it, snowed by it, is
the opposite, a balancing way of
    missing it

and yet
everything helps:
charts, voyaging, waiting quietly at
home, upon occurrence.

Discovery on Reading a Poem

One sail
opens the wideness to me of the waters,
the largeness of the sky.

Making Senses

Grey by water   fathering fallen
    gold by evening   or morning

gritty by cinder   or glass broken
    greasy by sliding   and sloping

singing by combers   silting slacking
sizzling by horseless   plastic and chrome

acrid by acres   at canal level

oakleaf smoky   at late sunlevel

sour at stoneboat   marsh-lily stalk
    AND
sweet by wicker   or water.

Choice

Walking
   in a rhythm like
   breathing, easy and
   mortally inescapable
into pre-sunrise
   (disappointingly) grey
   but (not disappointingly)
   past wet barley tips:

carnelian of birdsong vanishes.

Water bubbles invisibly under
   a mat of root and mantling turf.

A cold sour wind – in
   infancy, yes – but
   implicitly desolate, surf-livid,
   with the weird sting of newness
   on the wet skin, unsheathing eyes,
pours over land and around
   body as over a
   channel stone.

Far, now, steadily
farther into the cold ache, loss, submission to
walking-as-being – brief panics dart, at only
               wilderness and oneself:
one is accepted by Nowhere as its own.

   This
   must be forgone
   for the 'where'-asking, who
   is (in the convergences-suffering place still)
   dear.

The Unshackling

Locked in   in fear
that evening   where
ten were huddled   came
the eternal Lamb.

Two had seen gravecloths flat
in that emptied place.
All knew Mary had heard, had thought,
presence, voice, His.

Locked in   in fear:
'time's ebbed and we're alone:
how can we bear
the word that was life, then?'

He showed the torn
and holy flesh they knew
having come in
past door and bolt   right through.

'You, vulnerable (too),
with truth I breathe,
with My love, you can go
out (too). See, you are with

Me still.
Just as We will:
you will forgive,
receive.'

The bliss was quick, and brief.
'Then it's not *that* we feared!'
With their gladness and grief,
waiting, now, interfered.

Fierce, Old and Forest

Cold in the lead-broken sunset
waits the sandstrip
its pallor steady
in telescoped twilight.
Wet cedar branches and wet
black moss
breathe and stiffly
insects strut in sand-grass
                  ritual, unfleshed
                  figures of night-shore.

The Promise of Particulars

Foreign travel alerts
awareness, ice-sheeted, sore,
blurred.
For the first-stepping child
doorway at home or shore
of remote foaming sea – all, everywhere
burns with minutiae and risk and
wonder. For the spirit released,
too, all is
vivid, nothing
routine or lost to awareness,
and yet in that one-eyed
heart-whole wonder
tiny particulars will be
known within wholeness.
The late sun, spoking under storm
against prune-coloured stormclouds to the west
haloes and breathes among
the luminous leafless branchtips –
ivory, lilac, saffron, bronze (the
oaks against the rusting evergreen).
The moment winks, is gone.
But everything is shaped in prospect of the
glory.

Money Needs

Bread not eaten
becomes fur;
bread not eaten
grinds to dust.
Bread not eaten
in the rain,
bread not eaten, on
sunned stone,
are neither bread nor gain.

Words or doing, either, alone,
become stale bread
too long uneaten,
burdening us who gather now   to gather
bread, though all is spent.
Yet, sparrow-toed, hope comes
looking for crumbs, crumbs in the dust.

Sun-clocked priests baked fresh bread
and ate the almost stale bread.

We claim our stature all the same.
For us, through fire and air
is given life, in bread, and in
the need for bread. We will *in extremis*
escape hunger – and death.

Portrait of Karen Beaumont

I.

The quiet shine on the
long grasses pressed by the wind.

II.

deep   blue   water
sheered by the cliffs
white pines have cleft

III.

sparkling midnight
breathing full carnation
richness, Caribbean beautiful,
crimson   and midnight blue

IV.

January brook
bubbling under ice
and bubbling forth into the
sun-bewilderness, the
out there, here.

Thoughts on Maundy Thursday

His actions are
whole-hearted, clear, spontaneous,
and therefore can be
interpreted, after, as
purposeful too.

There are inherent beauties –
crystalline structures under microscopes* –
hidden in cliffs and canyons from our glance who
pick our way along there.

As, for instance, the sudden awareness
    while that supper was being served of
    their weariness, and of how refreshing
    cool water would be for friends not just put up with
    but loved in total vulnerability:
    mustn't it have been almost
    unbearable (the separating hour had come)?
    Then it would help simply to
    take the slave's towel and basin there.

O yes, it was an 'example', and a sign.
But more. The cliffs and canyons
are mine as well as the
equipped geologist's, just as for him
    more intricate structures
    are hidden still till the magnification
    comes, in glory.

---

* This is a reference to Violet Anderson's photomicrographs of crystals;
see the colour plates in *Monteregian Treasure: The Minerals of Mont
Saint-Hilaire*, Quebec, ed. J.A. Mandarino and V. Anderson (Cambridge
University Press, 1989).

Each time we fail
he sees our need and nerves himself
by telling us again
the way the Son of Man
must go.

Lord, make us vulnerable too, to love.

Godspeed

for Judy and Don MacLeod

Plunging about this city
shoring up cave-ins – ravine-bank,
garden, intersection –
until that caring, that reckless willingness
again opens reality – the one sure
Steadier, and the Foundation for newness –
for others now in their turn,

responsive, curious, free,
both of you, having opted for the best
            (among so many good
            'careers', able to meet their exactions
            and earn those rewards),
have found the best to be, often,
the buffeting, the neglect,
the corrosive committee hours,
absurdities, blame, demands,
the loneliest winter skies and
snow-light, after early morning prayer-meeting
or a vigil in ICU.

The Spirit steadied and cleared your spirits.

Now, though we are apart,
may He keep watch on our ways,
and continue to open your vistas, for you have courage,
on Truth and soreness, and glory.

When the Subway Was Being Built on Yonge Street

Pile-drivers whump.
          whump.
Day broke like a chunk
     of molar (i.e. brilliantly cold
                light/or pain)
     whump.

Is this our woods and larks and lovely
world to fit our
natures lovely in?

Carfenders. mirrors. milled dimes. manhole covers.
     whump.

By noon the trucks snow-churning and grinding
   by have hooked and chained our several eyes
      and wound us up on motor resonances.
     whump – whirr
     whump – whirr.

There is one response:
move? no, remain and prove
who all can wait it out.
These gaunt machines will fall
   silent, will
      be dragged away,
      gone!

The Banished Endure

A contour map misses
these fine-drawn quarters –
Babylon is gristle-dry
in from its waters and
the lulling fullness of the
silenced songs of Zion.

No watery skies
show on the papier-mâché maps.

The young have known no holy city.

Post stalks bald post; wired listeners
sing like mosquitoes.
                                    A mighty
river of dark swirls over
bird turret, blank bricked window.

The sinister unknown
binds, leg and arm,
in nightmarish paralysis.
Only awakening would bring release,
the knowledge that there is
a knower, though unknown.

'By the waters of Babylon ...'

Voluntarily in exile
here, among the destroyers of Jerusalem
       where we panic, indoors,
       or huddle by the wall
       hiccuping with distress, blind to all hope,
       or whirl among the whirlers
       or hack on at a root
       to keep the blinkers up against
             peripheral glares and dread,
You come, to be
unblemished, yet drawing all to
Yourself,
draining all but Your ways
    into the cup You purpose to drain for good
that the pure blood-sacrifice
might be forever made
turning all else tombward
till the invisible Temple shines
promising that terrible Day
and real walls, real courts, real glory
finally, rise.

Enduring

Trees wait their lifetimes
fragrantly   forthright
touching the night
and earthdeep
and my ear almost
speaks with them in the night
as I wait for the sounding
the long wind moves them to.

Tangle
risks itself in space
for contour's mysteries,
self-disclosure.

Some the sun stunts,
wind lopsides.
Love articulates the sunset-flooded
bark and arteries
deep rivers into
evening breathing.

Wooden. Yes. Cloth? –
torn in ragged mellow mornings
and sundering gales:
stark, delicate, deep-bosomed,
by turn
they wait their lifetimes.

A Small Music on a Spring Morning

Why did they put the
blue and white live
balloons out with the trash
this morning just because
the party's over – when they
thub on the cardboard still
roundly, and lift on their leashes?

Having balloons about on an
overcast morning is
celebration. O in the grey
nothing distracts from the bobbling
lightsomeness of a drift of
all-alone trembling to be touched
balloons.

The Word

Huge waterfalls in ever-travelling skies
sting us with their spray
in weeping eyes
even in our present shadow-form of day.

Prison to Fastness

We self-immured were plastic,
safe from both taint and air,
figured like truth and leafy growth
but fadelessly nowhere.

How levelly we saw it;
then we broke with keeps,
steadfast to search, no matter what,
all fars and highs and deeps.

We've burned a lot of gas and oil
and cooked on many a shore.
Whereall we've gone – and some we've seen –
long since began to blur.

The figurings of safety, growth,
have new their once appeal –
but not the plastic or the walls
on that ironic wheel.

To tolerate dissolves when all
are tolerating too!
The galaxy shoulders into night –
what 'in' there is, to go.

        (That frozen pigeon on the ramp,
        unnaturally defunct,
        has come by utterance   than ours
        more signally distinct.)

Comfy as gerbils on the loose
though cage and house begin
to chill – fires out and owner gone –
we nose for discipline.

Fade the eonic furnaces?
We're people nonetheless;
no gerbil knows such monster hope
as everyman's Loch Ness.

Moved by the source of all that moves
the mystery stirs unseen;
in nature so long missed he is
for us no might have been.

Wheatlight on tealblue morning,
Tulips dogeared by snow,
warn us with their loveliness of
our fastness out of now.

'He himself suffered when he was tempted' (Heb. 2: 18)

Yes, yes, we say, but exempted in
holiness, he didn't (as we do)
kid himself into range to get caught in the tempter's lasso.

He himself not only suffered
when he was tempted – though that a lover would
so choose to know what we know
protects and compels us somehow –

but think of the roped-in, rotten,
     welted and swollen, sick,
     tempter-take-all
     maggot-ripe end of our fall:

that too he chose. That suffering
was not to know what we know but so he
could instead of us; offering
(if we will love and let be)
in place of that, his glory
in holiness shared, claiming us as his family.

Beginnings

Each of us has
some sense of God
and we're all coping
with realities in our
life.
I have trouble getting the
two together.
You do too.
Everybody does.
Paul does.
In a sense he starts there.

The Cloud

The August storm
is tall as a wall.
How eerily the cosmos
unflutters like a feather
in this waiting stillness!

It Bothers Me to Date Things 'June the 9th'

for A. J. Stewart (who died June the 8th)

We put the dates in brackets,
the brackets closed, complete.
How can the life we share be there
when here is still a date?

A string of hours, left over:
it bothers us to know
we use this time our hearts refuse.
Shelterless, on we go.

To the all-knowing only one
all time is bared, at once.
The lovely then, the loss (for us)
remain, both in his glance.

How can we breathe the fragrance
of basswood, when to breathe
is not our common lot now?
Sorrow runs underneath

the lucite summer beauty;
this time is out beyond
time shared; we here are frozen and
eternity is   profound.

Can he share too in mortal time
who knows it closed, complete?
He knew the jolt of time gone cold
in Bethany, and wept.

He knows the powerful lack
hour upon hour
we want to fill with caring
now put beyond our power.

Because He knows us surely
with blessing and not blame,
help (dew-minute) is manna,
our stay, our strength towards home.

The Freeing

Unclasp my heart
though that disclose all:
you have known every part,
willing no-refusal.

Unclasp my heart
from my own cramped story
to new, in-threading light, a start
towards searching out your glory.

Unclasp my heart
to, unwithholding, close
on all that you impart
till daily life ensues
timeless, as you choose.

Cycle

Fear,
      threshold of every
      prayer – a
daring, never the
familiar trust, always
trust beyond
      the known.
      Waking to risks whets;
      venturing, sparks
fresh fear.

Our Only Hour

In the sunslick a shrub, its buds sealed in,
is skeleton'd in light. Sand clumps on
                    sand cast shadows.
Out of strange oceans day has unscrolled,
                    (low shining) has smoothed
        a HERE from among
farness and blueness and more, more, mounting and melting
                to indigo, and the centripetal
                    fires of gold.

His look was lightning.
The extraordinary angel
stood, where history cleft
BC – AD:
the keepers were as dead men.

    The keepers till the day they died
    could not forget. Blindness still stabbing, from the
        fierce glare of such a
        countenance (in the undwindling moment
                when they blacked out).

    Not everybody sees
    something like that in his time.
    And then can never
    distance it by
    words ('I always remember
        the morning …')
    Nobody could have heard.

    Often in the night
    the old keeper would
    butt again at the wall

of fact: the stone,
    the hurried debriefing to
        hide what was done
        and keep them each alone
        and dumb.

His look was lightning.

It is a disappointment
        to have seen
        the singular brightness and be
        only as dead men,
and then exist, later that day and on and on:
        the point of it
        searching you, idly now, somehow, in
        a gathering silence, a history
compulsively reviewed.

Could those keepers have actually
stifled the world?
One of them wondered,
waiting it out in the hours of his darkness.

        Three women were there.
        God kept them from terror.
        Truth shone, and shines.

The shrubbery by an apartment wall is
wire-bright in the keen north sun
        (sky jet-stream-sundered)
        and I think
        how it is the angel
        staggers belief.

Wide continents, telescope-swathed marine sky, our
   multifarious kind, spilling out, over, around:
   we receive 'all' easily but
   glimpse something, once or twice,
   which in our only hour will be
   massively known.

The angel, we
hardly expect,
can hardly credit.

But the man, torn, stained,
left in mummy-wrappings,
stone under stone?

the man then seen
alive, known
powerful, heard
in the heart's ear?

   He does not so stagger belief
   as overwhelm our grieving.

To a Fact-facer

When you crawled over the ice to the crest
and there was the deer the
wolves had torn
you had forbearance in the blast
    and blank of fear.

Now the candour of March is lit
and from the springing root
the liquors of life, stringbean sweet,
cry 'out!'

Now, bearing this with that
you make your winter time complete.

Open and Shut Case

He came right here – and we missed him.
Emptiness swallows us down.
He let us choose to hurt him.
He died alone.

His clarity and care –
oh, we heard and saw – and
twitched ourselves away.

The goodness we want should
be exclusive, not in our power
to even say no to.

He is here now.
Anyone's heart of stone
love loves to touch to
hurt and holiness.

Bolt from the Blue

When something ... split? – bright
terror, eardrum-crack,
conveyed, not the daylight
beyond sky's iodined mask

but the mask's volt,
discharge within the veil
(Zeus with his bolt
they used to envisage). For all

the here, and the out there
beyond all suns shining
God is alone. His fear
is the heart's inclining.

The I-wants in the Way

Your going off alone to pray
when all the sick were brought
though all were healed till night
drew us to sleep and you to pray ...
and then at dawn we thought
it would go on.... You taught instead,
and somewhere else.
        You pray
still. And we lean on what
seems 'ours', a healer, not
knowing the one who heals comes if you pray,
today, or in That Day – and not
because we clamour, but
as we too, trusting, learn to pray.

Then when you pray
we are alone
as you are, not alone.

To a Seeking Stranger

To a man who wants life to the full,
wants absolutely. Wants. For God's sake   yes:

in the milky blur of the day the Lord
has wakened me into, the long work and
the redolence the sun awakens (of
barnyard weeds, leaf smoke, snail moisture, bare rock)
I can forget that
stars burn, and emptiness coils among them
superbly, moiré-ebon, that you hear
always the gulpings of the night.

The sun in my sky has put out
your North Star. I go by.
You tell me.

A black storm suddenly plunges us
into a like turmoil. We both battle.
For God's sake yes.

What you asked for was
nothing but to know – enough.
Not the tiny somebody's sun
worked up like a dame's brooch to pin
cloth with.
Nothing from me certainly.
And to know yourself.

And yet
the man who lived, and died, but lives,
is judge of all the world. His
purity finishes us. And that
alive one blazons it: that he
is God – i.e.
perfect love, judging
for God's sake. Yes.

You, stranger, crushing
wax walls, honeycomb crushing
stranger, fervent for some
black, pine-cold pool, for
cleanness, and night's deeps,
in forest-savagery, obstructed
from completing that alone
being you know, and want to
know – enough:

you are game.
You know about an all-or-nothing throw.
You have told the truth thus far
to silence. Yes.

In time, farnesses
open. The bright large place
we must all need who would
be, begins to be.

The terrible, blood-guttering wood
can be everyday, too.
Yes.

Noted, Foundered

The tap of a carpenter's hammer
out on the lot.
The neighbour's tread on the tired stairs,
feeling her way, having bought
pinched loaves, waxpaper farmer's cheese, two chops,
stiffpaper sugar, wilt-paper greens, paperwet butter, and
the papers, trudging because she is hot.
These two pace the stutter and whir
of sewing-machine thought at its simple seam.

Somewhere a maiden spins in her prison in a tower.
She will endure for a hundred years but
she's licked from the start.

These are the masks of the midcontinent
where sea once moved, a seabed levelled, dried,
baked, abandoned, ours for this interim-ever.
Cities sprouted, bulged,
jostled for shine at sunset.
Rails and runways gleam and blink.

The carpenter still taps. The neighbour's aged parent
is dying in the civic hospital.

Priorities and Perspective

At eye level, abashed, I, this day
consent to think about Gethsemane.
In my hormonal youth the agony
was all I heard, and heard in terms of me.

Now a plain history is proving itself true
about Jesus's life, and not like me and you
but uniquely (still) raised from the three-day
tomb, and, still alive, keen to show us how.

No words, but on the Gospel page, no sign
of what it delegates now: his cross, and 'mine',
(he spoke of both). He sweats it out alone.
While we all huddle and slumber, it is done.

'No other way?' That's what at one point he said.
Step off the earth? that's hard – the earth he made –
why, see these very olive trees, each intricate
as is all simple being he created.

Plainly the options glared; eye level; he chose.
His struggle then would not be much like ours.
We twist away from the familiar as
stranger reality draws us, and draws us close.

To opt for wholeness God's way, by being killed
while the conundrum continues, of love felt,
though our unholy ways, on him, repelled
love and left him abandoned, to endure
so that we could be healed....

O, easy to theologize this, drive
it fast across the horizon, and believe
afar, yes, marvelling and moved – above
the ground of where I am and how I live!

Nothing like those cosmic priorities comes
my way. It seems that sanity comes
from being in proportion. And this day's bright sky comes
as context. To the minutest part, still energy comes.

> At Jesus's word the paralysed man stood
> and walked, forgiven, empowered.
> It was for 'authority given to men' the crowd
> in awe praised God!*

---

* Matt. 9: 8

... the Wound

Flame touched the marsh-grass,
withered harsh blades; and the flinch
of air and burning gas
smudged and leapt to a blue-lit
marsh-fire, ruddy at ground level.
Nests burn. Tough protectors' pinions
are singed and set down
crooked in the swelter.
Blue sky of August
burns with far cold fires.
Star-remote clear high
crystalline sun-thrust
spangles the tears
of marsh-island strangers
safe in their boat, safe in the river,
their water-bottle here
but their eyes smarting,
their bodies afloat as though empty
as though left desolate too.

For bpn (circa 1965)

The sign on the Library shelves tells it:

LANGUAGE HAS BEEN MOVED.

Look.
Sure enough.

        Has been moved over?

      (Don't jam in here –
whoever you are, here
where Language isn't ...)

        No.
        been moved deeply.

The park fountain is lost, lost
in the pitch-and-toss summer shower.

Our Travels' Ending

The sun went down just west of Utica;
lifting above the smoulder: a new moon.
The little waters in the bush
lay brown and still, although a puddle
on the mid-boulevard-grass-place mirrored
the light-washed zenith.

∽∽∽∽∽∽∽∽∽

Fish-skeletons, angel ones, shine,
or, scattered further, are just
smoky simulacra.
Now with the blackening of the ground cover
a richer platinum is the,
earlier, papery, moon.

∽∽∽∽∽∽∽∽∽

Life is no longer with the living forms.
The last light, tinted, lingers
while berry and twig, distinct, out of the dark,
are etchings only.

∽∽∽∽∽∽∽∽∽

O, now the moon is pumpkin gold
over the blue and fluorescent-tube
geometry of the toll booth.

∽∽∽∽∽∽∽∽∽

A maroon tinge, low, is all
that's left of day.

To Joan

The pulpit led a prayer:
'Thank God who brought us here.'

I prayed, 'We couldn't come unless
Joan came by car for us:
help me tell truth in this
while praying thus.'

The power of kindness, providence, skill,
derive from Me whose power is over all.

The act of God is found
lovely for being through my friend,
nonetheless His because
blessings, in her (through whom), also make final pause.

The Cursed Fig-Tree:
The form not the purpose of the parable

(Mark 11: 12–14, 19–26)

It seemed on the surface:
'I'm hungry. Give fruit' and, foiled, You let curses
dry up its root!

But that wasn't Your way.
Peter spoke up.
He'd heard You say
the tree's life would droop.

If it had been a curse
for desired figs failing
Your faith would be – and ours –
belied by Your 'desiring'!

For no fruit when the time
was wrong for fruit, its end?
Then? When Your time had come
but men would not respond?

Then, to teach us faith?
The mountain would remove:
our fears, resistance, earth-
bound 'life' that cost Your death.

And You highlight: forgiving
not practising spite,
and promises thriving
though still out of sight.

Might that tree help Your friends
know how You *could* vanquish
all those at whose hands
You preferred anguish?

They forgot when grief smote
who was King. But we see
how forgiveness and fruit
now depend on that Tree.

'Don't Touch the Glory'*

A flower opened in the air,
its sheath an opalescence,
pure white petals, golden fair
the fragrant heart, the terrible pure
fragility its essence.

'I can do nothing of Myself' –
the Son put off all claiming.
The Father takes all Judgment off
and gives His Son His suffering, Life –
and us ('our' Father naming!).

The Spirit, Jesus's, in us
prompts, heals, suffers rejection,
breathing in stillness, dim with grace
to wake us to that loveliest face
and Holy resurrection.

A trembling flower in our air
appears all fragrantly:
each Person subject by the power
of love, and each One perfect through
total humility.

Pride is the enemy. This One
who loves, this Trinity
is giving, yielding, making known
what glory is, and what alone,
tuning our praise and joy.

---

* This title is borrowed from a poem I read in a borrowed periodical
  years ago and have not been able to track down.

The flower burns on in the heart,
fragile, timeless, pure,
timeless There, here in soil and hurt
still working out His beautiful art
of Self-effacing power.

The Singular

Lord let us learn from you
not to deny the glory
of God in man
and never to glory in that except one man
releases glory again
by his amen.

On this bedrock glory
the humble homestead rides where
you serve, a willing slave.
You demeaned yourself
to inglorious us
once, for that Sabbath eve
when the light died.

  Glory is One
  only, is shared
  when set aside
  to share for good
  the only singular good.

Piercing the bedrock
on the first morning then we learn
that his Amen
breathes and will shine
in time to everyman
the glory of the One.

From Christmas through This Today

THE Light became our darkness
We rejoiced.

We found we were exposed
and were bemused.

Pointed to Light, the contrast we disliked, we
would have suppressed
the light but He rejoiced Himself to quench it
with all the worst.

Then from the tomb the terrible light
outburst
emptying all we'd gained and He
had lost.

The light that seeks us out
is as at first
but darkness now is different, only ours
by choice.

Child of our years, still help us till we know
the Lamb the only Light.

Self-mirrorings

Some few do hound and hit.
Most though protect, and will
shelter and help the hurt:
we're not bad, all in all.

> (One hit? one cries
> 'which one?' – O sore hearts then!)

In accidents and crises
of pain, passersby call
emergency services
and wait: don't we do pretty well?

> (Corporate coping shelters
> us maybe, more than them?)

Watch a child with a doll
stroke the imagined hurt,
comforting, hugging – all
care: isn't this our spirit?

> (This soothes the powerless rage
> of the real hurt
> even though then it was assuaged
> by being rocked quiet.)

YOU MEAN THAT THERE'S NO GOOD IN US AT ALL?

No, no. But that

> we're not much better than Peter was or
> naked John Mark, that night –
> nor for the fearsome next three days –
> nor through the shaken wonders afterwards.

Only the fiftieth day and the light poured
from somewhere not of us
does any good – if once

the uselessness of all the rest is glimpsed.

Oh, None of That! – A Prayer

From the namby-pams
of the cloaking faith I wear
deliver me. From the times
peculiar persons, particular people-swarms
seem not, to me, familiar;
oh, from the namby-pams that evade
the absolute scrutiny
and evade healing, oh, deliver me.
Whatever I read or hear or see
only declares what is in me,
an ominous freight
hidden – and worse let out.
But from an omnibus
contrition, burying
the sting of shame, of naming it,
deliver.

And from the pride in having none
('I'm like that' or 'Leave me alone,
I'm a dog, I'll worry this bone')
deliver me.

Goal Far and Near

sliced clear   water-wedge-shape
at sand-slope
welters as he wades.

He plunges, arrows the bright
channel between
beach, and, over there,
funnels and freight sheds and
minglings towards metamorphoses.

Swimmer becomes
bedaubed, shoves soggy crusts and
duck-feathers, chin lifted, among
prows, bricked wallfronts, iron
moorings ...

(are there ladders? is there
                someone to let one down?)

The sun bronzes the lurching dock-glum water
as deep below footways
as the plane on take-off glints
up beyond dock level.

Arrival is survival,
in fact, rescue.
Too remote now, he knows, that sand-spit he
so easily slipped off from.

Peace and War

A sharp-chinned boy
in the automat
tried the ice-cream bars
but none came back
though his coin went in.
He asked at the counter.
Said the counter-man, No,
I've got bars in the freezer
but I'll not hand one over
till you pay me too.

Should the boy go away?
Who should say should?
What makes the counterman so mad?

Power

Master of his first tricycle,
pedalling furiously towards the singing
lethal traffic
he – double elation – meets
his father fresh afoot from that main thoroughfare –
                to circle and
                come too? No – a palaver
in reasonable terms he mutinously
waits out, stubbed between lawn and father's foot,
all dammed-up and high voltage
with ears for where he'll go
only.
At last dad hoists him, waist under one arm
trike dangled from the other hand
and heads home.

DON'T PICK ME UP! the scarlet
struggling sobbing adventurer
wails (after the fact).

One is so powerful.
One is so small.

How can power know
not to make helplessness
what is decisive?

Wrong Word, Because Language Has to Be Also Human

The 'anger' of God?

I could not do without
some powerful yank, when I'm caught off guard in the
drift, the undertow,
the weed-mass,
the sudden hole in the shore's
rock-shelf cleft down to the
cold all-but-total dark.

'Anger' –
        our language
lacks words for what He knows
seeing us reckless of safeguards,

and knowing the beyond of 'total dark'.

Such seeing, knowing,
finally touches us

until one of us wants to
wriggle clear of some communal woe,
or misconceives response
as new-won innocence.

Then 'anger' makes us tremble
once again?

But He it is whose Spirit
transfigures faith into
love-neighbour-as-self,
seeing the potential He imparted
and, oh, expectant, loving that
(drastic with everything obscuring it).

In practice, will one oneday know
how so to love and
so to know distortions and contaminants
with such for love's sake anger?

Nothing Else For It

Seeing this we
fall to our knees.

We wouldn't be willing
to stop being persons
as he became willing
to stop being wholly
of light unapproachable
to become human
and die as a helpless
  animal died
  in the Jewish rite
  so that its drenching
  blood could besprinkle
  what needed cleaning.

How can we grasp it?

Being human
what can we do
but bow, and believe
now, or when glory
leaves all he made
transformed, or stricken.

Heavy-hearted Hope

Hope's not an emotion,
as *agape* is not.
It is a firm condition
established by one absolute hurt
till the encompassing joy – and that
only for walkers-not-by-sight, each one
in a deliberate devotion.

You grow by going towards?
Yes. Also: growing cells
are the most vulnerable
to cancer.

Pain comes   to see
unknowing (awe) not   keeping
wild growths of what we think we know
in check. Do we replace a living
with our own fictive person?
Are we forestalling even
hope then?
O, can we err so far?

Heaviness. Fear comes too.
Chernobyl's children are
ours, too, though out of reach,
probably walking still by sight,
dying probably.

No magic banishing
of consequences comes
though they strike only some, and we
are free still.
Hope is not wish-fulfilment.

My hope, not theirs, makes me
look to You more than ever
for hope.
May Your own grieving heart
instruct my cry.

The Touch of the Untouchable

O vulnerable
one whom I hurt
sorely, who never are victim,
whose going under
to the ignorant, crude, the
victim of self-tyrannies
goes under and on and
out into that brightness
that is our hope,

your compassion
sweeps like the autumn-willow-wind
into the damps of my
dimness, with
fresh stinging rain, a breath
sky-wide clean soft blowing
with cedar sweetness,
a promise of the sharp
lapis lazuli, star-studded
autumnal night.

Incentive

One walked the roads, slept
on a boat-cushion, waited alone
in enemy country at blazing noon for
water even,
paced it out to the end
in such clear strength

that (cows of Bashan
      slaking our thirst, calling for more,
      squashing poor people and not even noticing
      and on the right days all in good order
      sailing down aisles, heaping up
      flowers on the altar etc.)
we look to him for

?no bread
no rain
leaf-shrivel and pests and
fevers and sores and
violence?

would but these bring us back to
the footpaths and open
skies among night-breathing olive trees,
back to the waiting,
the hope.

Loss

Back window with red-checked oilcloth on the sill
and orange-red geraniums the leaves wrinkly
in sunlight, root-cellar boards, a clothesline,
lower fence caving valleyward where the worn
grass and feathery vegetable plot give way to
butter-and-eggs, among some bluish
perennial sweet peas:
the place is bared. Trees are long gone,
and the clutter of children gone
and the sun washes in to the bone.

Here pain hit home.

Its home makes the plain place
invisibly surge with beauty, almost unbearable
while it is day.

Out

My friend sleeps on
a day off, using
sleep as a refuge.

Our friend works over-
time, using work
as a refuge.

I see that I have used
the holy given as
my way of refuge.

The urgent hope drove him
stumbling, once,
away, past any refuge
although towards joy.

Forgive.
Be thou
alone our refuge.

Nostrils

Hay fever is a parody
of my extreme anxiety:
I fear that I may cease to
breathe. Yes. And I know
it will be so.

As a child in the forest once, I tried
to hold my breath, rehearsing so that I'd
be ready for my act;
but flesh made will retract,
and day resumed what had but briefly blacked.

Up-and-down   in-and-out   are passing strange
that they can make me be, oh, and can change
to immobility, rhythms' end,
as oceans tend
to surge and slack against quick air and land
though still where they're profound.

Than sense and pulses, so much more
waits, once one may explore.

Knowledge of Age

Knowledge of age
begins in winter, a thin-railed whistling gate
under sonorous pines
a few shivering paces, and so far,
from the stone house and all its hearths.

A slow slow seethe
of snow across banana branches is
illumined on a silk of sky
distinctly green, although no arch is there.
  On endless terraces of wine-stained space
  only plump cherubs play.

One afternoon bruised as November
in the triangular park nine small suede reindeer
feed on green moss. And city's heaven sunders to a
swift appropriate blue.

Summertime of other times shrivels
carbon and unmemorable now.

Anatomist, mark 'alive' this bone
that racks and sings in winter's gate
under sonorous pines.

The Ecologist's Song

Sometimes, where once the sky bent brown
above a creased doeskin of new earth
pillars plunge upwards, and through the thinning air
the pelting hail sweeps down.

Absorbing, glittering, the beach at noon
welters with silence. There a separate pool
has formed, plum-coloured, richer than water, cool,
shadowed by stillness in the naked sun.
A sudden gust whisks a gold shower
of stinging sand on the dark sheen.

Who brings the petals, cupped and shyly white?
Why are they bruised?
Who glassblows dew shaking the droplets out
to burn in icy leaf-tip and grass-blade
clear of the clustering wood?

Everywhere's ocean of sun, late-flowing, knows
the dark tides too, the netted shores
of land and air wrapping the lovely planet
round, and one knot of the net
loosed, one strand plucked in the net,
wake resonances through the hemispheres.

Attend. Attend.
In pool and sand and riffled waters, here is
significant witness of an event.

Learning Love a Little

Out from the murk over
blurred lake, from smoke-snuggled skyline
high, winks a jet (dot still), man-made light
giving the sky a
petal's pallor:
our craft, we know, yet
flower-strange.

The tinted trace
down the deep sky
curdling already, alerts
skin, temples, heart, to
receivingly wait upon
the evening:

therefore in the clattering
tunnel, in the subway car
hustled, borne, we are
strangers averted, and together.
Respect seeds the unbreathable air with
   a certain dotted-Swiss, a
      scent, and one dumbly welcomes
         this, and them.

Birthdays

Brambled-in peace, sky-smoking,
wild grass, and the thick springy grass:
this is the birthday-festal
star-correlated hour and place.

There on the green the two
shapely ivory-clear sun-dimmed
children shyly come
each from far off, in wonder.

'A birthday present for me?'
Shyly the gold and ivory said:
'you first ...' (perhaps too shy
to stir a step forward?).

'Here then' – and clay and ivory thrust
his present on the other little prince.

All the threads of the giver's
woven hidden heart
loosed (like the song of the warblers
in that place apart,

the glory of that garden)
and were all at once a bright
network, and all his being
hushed music, poised, alert.

The other prince, unravelled in a swift
plucking of beaks and cruel talons, was
torn into rustling space.

Black sprang from heart of sun.
Full morning bulged. The glare
faded the garden's delicate-spun
filaments. Landscape lay bare.

'A present, for *my* birthday?'
(numbly). He huddled, close
to the summer grass's bouquet
with its little hidden flowers,

and sighed, and stood. And there,
yes, gold and ivory – coming,
clear as before,
shy, his arms half hiding

his present (new and neverending
treasure, always undwindling,
never unsurprising).

From branch   sundrench   horizon
surging and faintly singing
musics awaken.

Thanks

This book was kept in process by two friends, Stan Dragland and Joan Eichner, both sensitive editors. Their discernment, orderliness, patience, oh and e-mailing, saw it through to completion. I cannot thank them enough.

Here I remember Kathleen Coburn (the Coleridgean) whose intervention, in England, got my first book out, *Winter Sun,* put together thanks to an eight-month grant (1956) from the Guggenheim Foundation. The late Denise Levertov, at Norton's request for six manuscripts, sought out mine (*The Dumbfounding*). William Pope produced the next two volumes (*sunblue, No Time*) as his own venture, then *Not Yet But Still* with help from the Canada Council for the Arts and the Nova Scotia Department of Education. I am grateful to all.

Acknowledgements*

Magazines:

Acta Victoriana, Applegarth's Folly, Blew Ointment, Canadian Forum, Canadian Literature, Canadian Review, Canadian Woman Studies, The Catalyst, Chatelaine, Christianity Today, Combustion, Compass, Desert Review, Ganglia, Ellipse, Evidence, Exile, Hermes, His, The Human Voice, Image, IS, Island, Kenyon Review, The Literary Review, The Michigan Quarterly Review, The New Quarterly, The New Reasoner, Origin, Poetry Canada Review, Poetry (Chicago), Presbyterian Record, Queen's Quarterly, Right on, The Second Mile, The (Toronto) Telegram.

Anthologies (in chronological order):

A. J. M. Smith, ed. *The Book of Canadian Poetry: A Critical and Historical Anthology.* Chicago: University of Chicago Press; Toronto: Gage, 1943.
John Sutherland, ed. *Other Canadians: An Anthology of New Poetry in Canada 1940–1946.* Montreal: First Statement, 1947.
Louis Dudek and Irving Layton, eds. *Canadian Poems 1850–1952.* Toronto: Contact, 1952.
Earle Birney, ed. *Twentieth Century Canadian Poetry: An Anthology with Introduction and Notes.* Toronto: Ryerson, 1953.
Bliss Carman, Lorne Pierce, and V. B. Rhodenizer. *Canadian Poetry in English.* Foreword by Lorne Pierce. Toronto: Ryerson, 1954.
Ralph Gustafson, ed. *The Penguin Book of Canadian Verse.* Harmondsworth: Penguin, 1958.
A. J. M. Smith, ed. *The Oxford Book of Canadian Verse: In English and French.* Toronto: Oxford University Press, 1960.
Eli Mandel and Jean-Guy Pilon, eds. *Poetry 62.* Toronto: Ryerson, 1961.

---

* This list has been revised and expanded from that printed in Volume One.

Ilona Duczynska and Karl Polanyi, eds. *The Plough and the Pen: Writings from Hungary 1930–1956.* Foreword by W. H. Auden. Toronto: McClelland & Stewart, 1963.

Milton Wilson, ed. *The Poetry of Mid-Century 1940–1960.* Toronto: McClelland & Stewart, 1964.

Claude Bissell, ed. *Great Canadian Writing: A Century of Imagination.* Toronto: Canadian Centennial, 1966.

Gordon Green and Guy Sylvestre. *A Century of Canadian Literature / Un Siècle de littérature canadienne.* Toronto: Ryerson, 1967.

Gary Geddes, ed. *20th Century Poetry & Poetics.* Toronto: Oxford University Press, 1969.

Gary Geddes and Phyllis Bruce, eds. *15 Canadian Poets.* Toronto: Oxford University Press, 1970.

Oscar Williams, ed. *A Little Treasury of Modern Poetry.* 3rd edn. New York: Scribners, 1970.

H. Houtman, ed. *Six Days: An Anthology of Canadian Christian Poetry.* Toronto: Wedge Publications, 1971.

Eli Mandel, ed. *Eight More Canadian Poets.* Toronto: Holt, Rinehart and Winston, 1972.

Homer Hogan, ed. *Listen! Songs and Poems of Canada.* Methuen Canadian Literature Series. Toronto: Methuen, 1972.

Richard Ellman and Robert O'Clair, eds. *The Norton Anthology of Modern Poetry.* New York: Norton, 1973.

Paul Denham, ed. Preface by Mary Jane Edwards. *The Evolution of Canadian Literature in English.* Toronto: Holt, Rinehart and Winston, 1973.

Robert Weaver, ed. *The Oxford Anthology of Canadian Literature.* Toronto: Oxford University Press, 1973.

Alvin Lee, Hope Arnott Lee, and W. T. Jewkes, eds. Supervising editor, Northrop Frye. *The Peaceable Kingdom.* Literature: Uses of the Imagination Series. New York: Harcourt, Brace, Jovanovich, 1974.

Carl F. Klinck and Reginald E. Watters, eds. *Canadian Anthology.* Toronto: Gage, 1974.

Herbert Barrows, Caesar R. Blake, Arthur J. Carr, Arthur M. Eastman, and Hubert M. English, eds. *The Norton Anthology of Poetry.* New York: Norton, 1975.

Cid Corman, ed. *The Gist of Origin.* New York: Grossman, 1975.

Gary Geddes and Phyllis Bruce, eds. *15 Canadian Poets Plus 5.* Toronto: Oxford University Press, 1978.

John Newlove, ed. *Canadian Poetry: The Modern Era.* Toronto: McClelland & Stewart, 1977.

Merle Meeter, ed. *The Country of the Risen King: An Anthology of Christian Poetry.* Grand Rapids, Michigan: Baker Book House, 1978.

Douglas Daymond and Leslie Monkman, eds. *Literature in Canada.* Vol 11. Toronto: Gage, 1978.

John Frederic Nims, ed. *The Harper Anthology of Poetry.* New York: Harper, 1981.

August Kleinzahler, ed. *News and Weather: Seven Canadian Poets.* Ilderton, Ontario: Brick Books, 1982.

Jack David and Robert Lecker, eds. *Canadian Poetry.* Toronto/Downsview, Ontario: General/ECW, 1982.

Margaret Atwood, ed. *The New Oxford Book of Canadian Verse: In English.* Vol. 11. Toronto: Oxford University Press, 1983.

Donna Bennett and Russell Brown, eds. *An Anthology of Canadian Literature in English.* Vol. 11. Toronto: Oxford University Press, 1983.

In Celebration, Anemos. Poems for Denise Levertov on her sixtieth birthday. Palo Alto: Matrix Press, 1983.

Robert Lecker and Jack David, eds. *The New Canadian Anthology.* Toronto: Nelson, 1988.

Gary Geddes, ed. *15 Canadian Poets x 2.* Don Mills, Ontario: Oxford, 1988.

David A. Kent, ed. *Christian Poetry in Canada.* Toronto: ECW Press, 1989.

Gary Geddes, ed. *15 Canadian Poets x 3.* Don Mills, Ontario: Oxford, 2001.

János Tarn and Katalin Thury, eds. *Kristálykert/Crystal Garden.* Budapest: Hungarian-Canadian Friendship Society, 2001.

Donna Bennett and Russell Brown, eds. *A New Anthology of Canadian Literature in English.* Don Mills, Ontario: Oxford University Press, 2002.

Sharon Thesen, ed. *The Griffin Poetry Prize Anthology: A Selection of the 2003 Shortlist.* Toronto: House of Anansi Press, 2003.

Robert Scholes, Nancy R. Comley, Carl H. Klaus, David Staines. *Elements of Literature, Poetry/Fiction/Drama.* Don Mills, Ontario: Oxford University Press, 2004.

Translations:

Branko Gorjup and Francesca Valente, eds. *Il cuore che vede/The Optic Eye.*
   Ravenna: Longo Editore, 2003.

Publishers:

Routledge & Kegan Paul, London, *Winter Sun,* 1960.
W.W. Norton, New York, *The Dumbfounding,* 1966.
McClelland & Stewart, Toronto, *Winter Sun and The Dumbfounding,*
   Poems 1940–66, 1982.
Oxford University Press, Toronto, *Selected Poems,* 1991.
Lancelot Press, Hantsport, Nova Scotia, *sunblue,* 1978; *No Time,* 1989;
   Not Yet But Still, 1997.
Brick Books, London, Ontario, *Concrete and Wild Carrot,* 2002.
The Porcupine's Quill, Erin, Ontario, *Always Now: Volume One,* 2003.

Index of Titles

Margaret Avison was born in Galt, Ontario, in 1918. She studied at the University of Toronto, and subsequently worked as a librarian, editor, lecturer, and social worker. She has twice been awarded the Governor General's Award (for *Winter Sun*, 1960, and *No Time*, 1989). She holds three honorary doctorates, and has been named an Officer of the Order of Canada. Her most recent collection of poems, *Concrete and Wild Carrot* (Brick Books, 2002), was awarded the Griffin Prize for Poetry. It also received the Jack Chalmers Poetry Award from the Canadian Authors Association.